The Future of the Metropolis: People, Jobs, Income.

Edited by
ELI GINZBERG

Olympus Publishing Company
Salt Lake City, Utah

This report was prepared for the Manpower Administration, U.S. Department of Labor, under research contract number 21-36-73-37 authorized by Title I of the Manpower Development and Training Act. Since contractors performing research under government sponsorship are encouraged to express their own judgment freely, the report does not necessarily represent the Department's official opinion or policy. Moreover, the contractor is solely responsible for the factual accuracy of all material developed in the report.

Reproduction in whole or in part permitted for any purpose of the United States government.

HT
123
F89

Contents

4

Foreword

The imbalances in our large cities between the capabilities of those who seek jobs and the jobs that are available, between the location of the available jobs and where people live, between the pulling and hauling of different interest groups and the need for a consensus to assure the continuing viability of the metropolis, between the demands placed on local government and the financial resources and other powers which are primarily in the hands of federal and state governments — these and other tension points lie at the core of the urban dilemma.

This book represents a cooperative undertaking among a group of social scientists who seek to illuminate the major forces that have brought our cities to their present state and to suggest how these cities can gain control of their future. The contributors are from diverse disciplines — urbanology, demography, management, economics, public finance, the study of minorities, and manpower — but they share here a common focus on the interfaces of manpower and the metropolis, and they move easily between analysis and policy.

The book is an outgrowth of an earlier collaboration between the Conservation of Human Resources Project, Columbia University, which sponsored the conference at Tarrytown, New York, in November 1973, for which the several chapters were prepared as working papers, and the Office of Manpower Research and Development, U.S. Department of Labor, which provided the funding.

5

The last chapter is the direct outgrowth of the lively interchanges among the authors and the participants at the Tarrytown conference who were informed persons from a wide variety of urban groups: management, labor, minorities, government officials, planners, academics.

Dr. Howard Rosen and Mr. Joseph Epstein, of the Office of Manpower Research, and Professors Dale Hiestand and Thomas Stanback, Jr., of the Conservation staff, played an active role in the design and execution of the project. Mrs. Anna Dutka of the Conservation staff oversaw all the details connected with the Tarrytown conference.

In preparing the final manuscript for printing and in seeing it through galleys and page proofs, I was greatly helped by Alice M. Yohalem of the Conservation staff.

Eli Ginzberg, Director
Conservation of Human Resources

Columbia University
November 1974

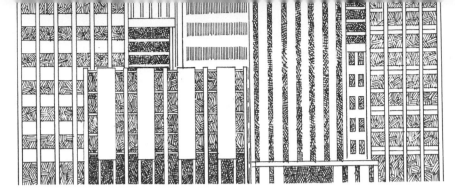

1
Emerging Issues in Metropolitan Economies

Wilbur R. Thompson*

One objective of this chapter is to find some tenable middle ground between a routine description of "what is" in the large metropolitan area of today and wild speculation about "what might be" in the "city of the future." Because this chapter has the serious charge of providing a base for our discussions of trends and issues in the large city labor markets, it seemed important to inventory at least briefly much that we all have learned through casual observation — what we know in common. But this standard fare is enriched with more than a little disciplined speculation about the near future. If later pages are a little more speculative than disciplined at times, this does not seem to be an inappropriate bias for an effort that is seeking multiple ways to increase knowledge.

The approach is to consider first the metropolitan area as a whole, preserving the useful fiction that it is a single, indivisible, local labor market, and taking the positive position that in general, bigger is better. Next, the growing subdivision of that local economy into subeconomies and labor submarkets is discussed, beginning simplistically with a duality of central cities and suburbs. Then the outlook for the central city is reviewed in a variation on an old theme: The King is dead; long live the King! Finally, time and space are brought center stage by re-viewing the city as an aging stock of capital, destined to recycle one day or another, one way or another.

---

* Professor of economics, Wayne State University.

THE LARGE LOCAL LABOR MARKET

A discussion of the nature and development of the metropolitan area as a local labor market might best begin by our calling attention to the very real and substantial advantages of large size, before we pick away at its shortcomings. We did not, as a nation, come to live in large metropolitan areas solely because of their benefits to us as consumers. Nor do we rejoice in the efficiency of their public sectors. As much as anything, large cities offer: (a) steady work, (b) good jobs, (c) occupational choice, (d) occupational ladders to better jobs, and (e) a better balance of bargaining power between employer and employees.

Larger city size brings more separate establishments (employers) and more different industries. A large number of employers contributes an element of stability to the local labor market by protecting the workers (and the local economy) against errors, weaknesses, and simple misfortunes of individual entrepreneurs or managerial groups—poor design, a misjudged market, inadequate financing, or just the luck of the draw. Having sheer numbers on the buyers' side of the labor market also serves to equalize bargaining power over the price and conditions of work. Much of the early and most fundamental defense of unionism was premised on the distorted image of the labor market in the "company town." More broadly seen, alternative employment nearby becomes especially important when joined to other social goals, such as working-class home ownership. Labor economists point out that home ownership reduces the *spatial* mobility of workers; but urbanists would respond by pointing out that residing in a large metropolitan area makes it possible to change jobs without having to move, much less having to migrate, and makes it highly probable that such job changing will in fact occur.

Larger city size also brings industrial diversification, a good hedge against sharp cyclical slumps and against prolonged secular decline of old industries. Diversification — a representative mix of industries — does not of course promise local *cyclical stability*; rather, it offers only the middling prospect of average fluctuations from a national cycle — a kind of fail-safe. But diversification does offer the prospect of *seasonal stability* by matching offsetting winter and summer peak demands for labor. And industrial diversification through large city size is the surest path to *growth stability* (a) over the next decade or two by mixing new and old industries and income-elastic and -inelastic products, and (b) even beyond into the distant future by generating the infrastructure that ensures the continuing birth of new industries (e.g., centers of research and development, deep pools of risk capital, and forums for the clash of ideas).

Industrial diversification also implies occupational variety, and this opens the way to fuller employment, higher job satisfaction, and human development. Occupational variety makes it much more likely that there will be unskilled jobs for the uneducated; part-time jobs for students, the semiretired, and female heads of households; and light work for the elderly and the handicapped. Widening choice also increases the probability that one can find a job that is both interesting (or at least relatively tolerable) and a vehicle for self-expression. Diversification also creates "occupational ladders" that give real meaning to on-the-job training as an alternative to formal schooling. Finally, only big cities are likely to provide the wide range of occupational choice that makes it possible, even probable, that both an educated husband and his educated wife will be able to find suitable employment — labor in "joint supply." Nothing beats big cities as pluralistic workplaces for individuals and as efficient labor markets for the nation.

Industrial Filtering and Occupational Hierarchies

Standing back a little from the details of industrial location and regional development, one can see the broad outlines of a national pattern of "industrial filtering" (Thompson, 1968). With a new process to be mastered, new industries are most often launched in the older, larger, and more sophisticated industrial centers where work skills are highest, risk capital easiest to find, and diverse and even esoteric technical supports — specialized laboratories and professional specialists — most accessible. The question in the early days is: Who can do the job? But in time the question changes to: Where can the job be done the cheapest?

With time and production experience come the rationalization and routinization of the maturing industrial process; and as the aging industry slides down its "learning curve" toward ever lower skills requirements, it seeks out — is competitively forced to find — cheaper labor markets. Languishing farm service centers, in rural hinterlands where there is serious underemployment and new economic bases are being desperately sought, stand out as pools of cheap labor. Raw farm labor can rise to the modest demands of simplified factory processes. Besides, the congestion and high taxes of big cities are an unnecessary cost for simple operations that do not need big city facilities.

A filtering down theory of industrial location goes far toward explaining the common lament of the isolated small town: Why do we always get the slow-growing and poorly paid industries? Small places find that they must run to stand still because their industrial "successes" seem to come to these out-of-the-way spots only to die. These industrial backwaters also struggle in vain to raise per capita income, hobbled by industries that pay at or near minimum wage rates. Simple operations, low wage rates, and slow growth are the hallmarks of the aging industry. Both the larger industrial centers from which and the smaller places to which industries filter down *must* run to stand still at the national average rate of growth in employment and population, or so it would seem. The larger places do, however, run for higher stakes.

The filtering down of industry is easy to perceive intuitively, easy to rationalize deductively, and easy to illustrate selectively. Rigorous demonstration and precise quantification of the relevant magnitudes and timing suffer for lack of good data. We need to know whether the flow of the older, simpler manufacturing work is welling up or drying up, whether it is trickling down farther or less far, and whether its rate of descent is speeding up or slowing down.

The dilemma of the small town is that the farther down it is on the industrial ladder and the lower its skills and wage rates, the longer it takes for a given industry to get there, and the greater the risk that it will never arrive. Many industries do not in fact descend more than a few city-size steps before they: (a) fade away, (b) stabilize in location, (c) become transformed through technological change into more sophisticated activities and climb back upward, or (d) filter down and right out of the country to much lower wage labor markets, such as the Orient.

The somewhat less crucial, but still socially significant problem of the large metropolitan area, sitting on the top of the heap of the national stockpile of skills, is that it tends to suffer a lack of low-skill work. If industries do in fact age, become simplified, and filter down through the national system of cities, then human resources would tend to filter up through that hierarchy in a complementary way, with the more talented persons moving to the more advanced areas. The textile towns of the Piedmont area have been able to maintain full employment of a rapidly expanding labor force — have been able to absorb the exodus from agriculture in that region — by capturing an ever larger share of these slow-growing industries. But tight local labor markets have not closed the income gap because many of the more ambitious and talented young adults of that region have migrated out and filtered upward to various larger places. Worse still, this trading of high talent for low-skill work has compromised the long-run development of that region by draining off future leaders and potential entrepreneurs.

This is, moreover, a double-edged sword in that the larger, more industrially sophisticated urban areas of the North, rich in talent, struggle with heavy unemployment that leads to near unemployability for lack of enough low-wage, unskilled work. The New York City labor market, with only slightly less than its share of the less talented and underprivileged, needs low-skill work as desperately as a textile town needs high-skill work. In addition, this excess supply of marginal labor is not likely to be relieved by outmigration because low-skill work is not all that plentiful anywhere. Besides, the relatively generous welfare payments in New York are five to eight times as high as in the South, and may be nearly as high as low-skill wages in milltowns. Again, superior "free" public services in New York City (i.e., education, recreation, and medical and other health services) and the cost of moving away impede the outmigration of the poor.

In general, if natural increase tends everywhere to produce a population with a normal distribution of talent and ambition, and if industrial filtering tends to separate high- from low-skill work in distant labor markets, then massive migration is dictated. But if the more talented, motivated, and educated are the more mobile, the net flow is biased toward the larger, higher skill places.

The policy options here are not all that clear. Still, at the very least we should take great care not to obstruct unnecessarily the employment of low-skill workers in the industrially advanced, high-skill, high-wage, large urban areas by imposing minimum wage laws or uniform work standards, or any other devices, in such a clumsy way that we make employment of low-skill workers uneconomic. Let us struggle with hard-to-administer public subsidies to employers, if it is necessary to keep minimum wage laws to avoid cutthroat competition in labor markets. Would minimum wage laws still be necessary under an adequate program of family income maintenance, such as a comprehensive negative income tax?

INNER CITIES VS SMALL TOWNS

Almost unnoticed, central cities of large metropolitan areas and remote small towns have become natural rivals in a life and death struggle. Both places tend to house workers of low skills and poor general education, and both places must still cope with a continuing, although slowing influx of migrants who also lack job experience and work discipline. Yet central cities and remote small towns have great need for substantial amounts of low-skill work, and at a time when the national economy is experiencing a shortage of such work. A decade ago, manpower analysts and forecasters warned that "automation" would eliminate jobs for the unskilled and semiskilled faster than rising levels of general education and manpower programs hurriedly put together would empty the ranks of such workers. Even if the threat of automation now seems in retrospect to have been much overstated, or at least the time required for major displacement of labor was much understated, the thin, hard core of that exaggerated fear has now been reinforced by mounting concern over the rapid rate of worldwide industrialization.

With virtually all of our radios and more than half of our television sets imported, and with the even more sophisticated production of automobiles and other machinery slipping out of the country to be manufactured elsewhere, we have in effect been adding tens of millions of (foreign) workers to the domestic labor market. Moreover, to the extent that we are exporting advanced technology through patent licensing and the direct investments of multi-nation corporations, we move the cutting edge of foreign labor competition to ever higher levels of skill. Insofar as displaced domestic workers of medium skills are willing to accept lower skill jobs, lower skill workers are much more than proportionately subject to unemployment and relegated to the welfare rolls by the increase in foreign trade.

If there is indeed a large and growing shortage of low-skill work, do we not care where that scarce work becomes located? And if so, where would we have it located? In small towns? In inner cities of large metropolitan areas? Or in some other place? Only the federal government would seem to be in a position to weigh the full social costs and benefits of alternative locations and to avoid the worst excesses of cutthroat competition for industry. But if one federal authority acts to attract low-skill work to remote small towns (in the name of "urban and rural balance") while another federal authority acts, through a separate and uncoordinated program, to attract that same work to inner city ghettos (in the name of urban redevelopment, sometimes called "Black Capitalism"), we will find ourselves maneuvering and spending too little or to no net effect — robbing Peter to pay Paul.

We might opt for channeling low-skill work more toward some select set of small towns (e.g., "growth points") for any one or more of a number of reasons. The cost of simple living may be lower in small towns — or more likely, in small cities — raising the *real* wage of the lowest paid group. And if we come to a national strategy that encourages welfare families to live in low-cost places, it would be supportive to have an ample supply of simple work within easy access of potentially employable adults and to have entry jobs ready for their children. Or we may believe that unskilled workers prefer the small-town life-style, raising further their real (psychic) income. We should take care here because, while WASPs feel at home in the countryside, blacks, chicanos, and other minorities more often prefer city life. Again, various supportive services for welfare families may be more effective in small places, even if less professional. Finally, we may use this work and these people as instruments (pawns?) to preserve small places through the difficult transitional period while awaiting some delayed but still expected event that will revitalize those places.

As is all too often true, the opposing case is equally impressive. Inner city areas have the strength of being labor submarkets that overlap in space and offer possible, if sometimes difficult, access to other higher skill submarkets in the suburbs and satellite cities nearby. Even long journeys to work in other labor submarkets in the outer ring help ease and speed upgrading, compared to the need to migrate that faces the ambitious unskilled worker in the small town. Being able to change jobs without migrating — without even having to "move" in most cases — is especially important when different members of the same household are moving up in job skills at very different rates.

When we look to the employability of the next generation, we see that it is an open question as to where the schools and neighborhoods are better. The central cities' museums and public libraries are generally superior, tipping the balance in their direction for the more academically inclined youth. But the more personal and humane environment of the smaller place may be a better environment for the vocational development of less confident adolescents — and intimidated adults.

Perhaps the strongest case for favoring the inner city in guiding the location of unskilled work arises from the advantages to minorities of sheer scale. A small town of ten thousand population would probably amass a black population of only five hundred to a thousand persons, not nearly enough to provide the market needed to support black institutions.

And black cultural expression may well be the key to a strong sense of individual identity that may, in turn, be the key to community development. The case for segregation favors inner cities as sites for low-skill work, just as the case for integration favors small cities — the principal locus of "naturally integrated" schools.

Or we could get the worst of both worlds. Because of a combination of the suburbanization of manufacturing, segregated housing patterns and urban sprawl, and the deterioration of the public transportation system, suburban plants are typically short of unskilled labor for routine operations. This acts to induce them to pick up and move to remote small towns, frequently in the South where unskilled, nonunionized labor is cheap and plentiful. Whether such a response should be counted as in the broader public interest is debatable . . . the inner city's loss is the small town's gain, and both places are hard pressed to survive in an economy which seems to favor heavily metropolitan area suburbs as sites of both new business and the best jobs. What is clearly *not* in the public interest is for suburban plants to adapt to the unskilled labor shortage in the suburbs by remaining in place and substituting capital for labor — "automating" simple operations — or substituting relatively scarce higher for relatively abundant lower skill labor.

Clearly, it would be a bitter harvest if we were to permit our land-use and transportation planning errors — weaknesses of the heart and will, as much as of the mind — to be turned into avoidable "structural unemployment." What possible justification can be offered for allowing our cities to develop in forms that so increase the "delivered price" of unskilled labor at the new and growing suburban workplaces that sub-marginal machines become economical replacements for manpower? At a time when we are critically short of unskilled work, both to reduce income inequality and to provide entry jobs as first steps to higher skills, there has been remarkably little discussion of our vital interest in preventing this work from bearing transportation costs that price it out of existence.

BIG CITIES MAY NOT GROW AND STILL NOT DECLINE

If an occupational and skills hierarchy does indeed exist, favoring the larger urban areas, and if because of this (and the excitement of big cities) the more able and ambitious do tend to migrate toward these larger places, bigger is indeed better in local labor markets, at least for the more skilled. And *growth* may not be crucial for *development* in the bigger cities. Ordinarily, a rate of local job formation at least equal to the rate of *natural increase* in the local labor force is needed to keep the labor market tight — to avoid unemployment and underemployment in the short run and adverse net outmigration in the long run. But it is more than possible that very large metropolitan areas can withstand rates of population growth that fall well below the natural rate of increase, and perhaps even down to zero, without seriously undermining the local economy.

Unlike a small city, which suffers a youth and brain drain under slow growth, the great city may offset the pressure of net outmigration with the very real advantages of sheer scale. The Pittsburgh metropolitan area had almost the same total population in 1970 as it did in 1960, but one might easily speculate that bright young men and women from all over western Pennsylvania and eastern Ohio and West Virginia still head for that nearest metropolis, still seek tryouts on so large and prominent a stage. Even in its present static state in numbers, Pittsburgh would still seem to offer the lure of money, visibility, and power — an arena for corporate lawyers, heart surgeons, television producers, and management consultants of every variety.

A thin stream of young talent still coming to town probably more than makes up for the much heavier outflow of semiskilled workers and middle-aged parents. In any event, Pittsburgh affords us our first example of zero population growth on a large scale, and in the broader context of a still significant, if slowing, positive rate of national population growth. Can big cities stand still in a growing nation, in total population, without deteriorating? Can we, without appreciable harm, slow the growth of great cities below their natural rate of population increase?

CENTRAL CITIES AND SUBURBS

The metropolitan area achieves its identity most clearly and can be delineated in space most surely as a local labor market. The economist in particular derives such great analytical power by beginning with this integral economic space that, quite understandably, he or she has been slow to review this judgment. Still, it is the economist who should take the lead in revising this oversimplified stereotype. A number of factors has combined to split the large metropolitan area into a small number of subeconomies which overlap enough to leave blurred boundaries but are still distinct enough to be identifiable and have important policy implications. (The overlapping of labor submarkets arising from the centrifugal growth of the city is separate from and additive to the over-lapping at the edges of urban areas because of the formation of great linear strips of cities — the "megalopolis.")

The decentralization of manufacturing began long before World War II, but this early trend was temporarily halted and reversed by war-time shortages that locked most of the rapid expansion in production of that period into prewar plants located in the big central cities. Then with the postwar release of building materials and the construction of new plants, old trends toward the suburbs and small cities were reestablished. Within two decades after the end of the war, the share of manufacturing employment held by the central cities of the larger metropolitan areas had declined from two-thirds to less than half. It is worth noting that this trend closely paralleled the suburbanization of population, almost as closely in fact as retail trade followed population to the suburbs — an association that was more apparent and seemed entirely logical. Data on the location of service employment are much poorer, especially of the professional services upon which city economies depend, but apparently such employment has remained relatively concentrated — perhaps two-thirds or more of firms staying in their old locations downtown.

In first approximation, the largest metropolitan areas seem to be evolving into at least two roughly identifiable subeconomies. The central city is becoming more a place of business, professional, and governmental services — the marketplace of management consultants, financiers, lawyers, and officials of every stripe. The suburbs are more and more the heartland of manufacturing. Retail trade and *personal* services are performed, nearly proportionately, in both places, convenient to their customers. These "dual economies" are tenuously bound together by the long-distance commuting of suburban white-collar workers heading toward downtown offices and passing blue-collar workers from the central city "reverse commuting" toward outlying plants, and female domestic service workers on their way to suburban residences.

But these ties of cross-commuting may be drawing thin as the money and time cost of the long journey to work stimulates a sorting-out process that draws home and work closer together. Suburban manufacturing plants offer middle-skill work that fits well the residential preferences of their workers. And given the combined power of labor unions and oli-gopolistic employers to raise wages and prices, average skills command above-average incomes to pay for newer than average homes in the suburbs. Thus the locational preference of most manufacturing plants matches the residential preference of most manufacturing workers, and coupled price power in labor and product markets has blessed this union. And this economic symbiosis is tightened by the dependence of the plants on trucks, the workers on cars, and their mutual dependence on low-density land use — "urban sprawl."

The *potential* for a drawing together of home and work exists in central cities, impeded by the long and difficult process of rebuilding the cores of old cities. Professional services, founded on frequent personal contacts, preferably face to face and without undue delay, still cluster in or near the old downtown and act as a magnet for in-town living of professional workers. If professionals on the whole enjoy the city more than, say, manufacturing workers, and if the former are more inclined to avoid long automobile trips to work, there is at least a strong *latent* demand among professionals for in-town living.

Low-skill, low-income, personal service workers have little choice but to rent the older housing of the inner city, near the best of a bad lot of public transit. At least there is convenience in their proximity to the stores and offices in which they work. (Admittedly, the direction of causation may be reversed: Inner city personal service workers may have low skills because they lack easy access to middle-skill manufacturing jobs in the suburbs. But most empirical work to date suggests that this latter is the ebbtide.)

A central location, near the hub of the public transportation system, is a big help in job hunting, a never-ending activity for those "last hired and first fired" and for those relegated to casual employment. In fact, personal service work, free of the production imperatives of the assembly line and the work rules of unionized employments, provides the richest supply of the part-time work sought by female heads of households, second earners in the family, the elderly, and the handicapped. Finally, public service employment, free from competitive pressures, has the *potential* to become a prime source of part-time jobs, and this work is located more than proportionately in the inner city and in the downtown area in particular.

DECLINE OF THE OLD DOWNTOWN

Students of the rise and fall of the central city became concerned first about the falling share of metropolitan area retail trade accounted for by the central business district — "the decline of downtown." On the average, central cities have seen their share of retail sales fall steadily from about four-fifths of the metropolitan area total in the early postwar period to about half today. But this trend loses much of its mystery and most of its ominous implication when it is compared to the parallel decline in central city population from about two-thirds of the metropolitan area total at the end of the war to about half today. If the decline in share of retail trade jobs has slightly outpaced the decline in share of population, this is not at all surprising when we remember that there is first a lag and then some catching up: It takes a little time to raise a set of suburbs to the threshold population needed to support the quantum jump to a regional shopping center.

The passing of old downtown as *the* retail trade center was of course inevitable; consider the natural history of the city. Cities, like trees, grow from their center outward. In time and with greater size, households near the edge of town come to be very far from the center, and downtown's advantage of having a head start is overcome ultimately by the friction of distance — and the quiet amassing of a suburban market large and rich enough to permit retail operations at efficient scale. And perhaps just as important, the mounting distance and scale have typically been accomplished in a time period slightly shorter than the normal depreciation (and replacement) period of the downtown stores and the surrounding inner city housing. Thus the rise of the bright new suburban shopping center comes typically at a time when the central city is in its "awkward age": too old to love but not too old to throw away. It was hardly a fair fight.

There were of course factors other than distance and scale, some favorable to the old center. The central business district has retained a larger share of daytime working population than it has of the resident population of the region, and it attracts a disproportionate share of the visitors to the region, both of which act to swell its share of selected kinds of retail trade. But to offset this, the natural market-shed of downtown, under competition from the suburbs, is the inner city, typically the poorest residential area. The other side of this badly worn coin is that middle-income families become reluctant to pass through the inner city into old downtown, some because of a fear of walking what they believe to be unsafe streets, and others who just find it unpleasant to have to cope with the traffic, the dirt, and the noise of that most intense part of the city.

The aging of the old downtown, and of the inner city in general, and the growing obsolescence of its form were disguised by ten years of acute

depression and five years of war, during which time very little new building of any kind — stores or houses — was put in place. From 1930 to
1945, no major relocation could occur; downtown's monopoly position
was artificially prolonged. But when finally the affluent could move out
into new houses and new commercial centers could be built, the out-
migrants left behind capital that had been used too long and too hard.
The suppression of the natural forces of aging, when released, caused an
impact more sudden and perhaps also more severe than would otherwise
have been true. This same period was of course also one in which a great
backlog demand for automobiles was being built up, the indispensable
complement to postwar suburban sprawl, and the natural enemy of
high-density downtowns.

The Role of Services

One would be hard pressed to find a prediction or speculation about
the future of the central business district that did not look with the
greatest hope to the service industries. A rough working estimate of the
trend in the central cities' share of service work is that a modest decline
took place from the early postwar level of from 80 to 90 percent across
the various services to a current range of 70 to 80 percent of metropolitan area employment. This is clearly a remarkable job retention rate
for the central cities, given their much sharper decline in population
share from about two-thirds of the metropolitan area number to about
half over that same period.

(Critical comment is frequent on the lack of good data on the intra-
urban location of workplaces and jobs, especially in professional services.
But just as troublesome is the fact that the data are most often reported
by political subdivisions. The boundaries of "central cities" are, for purposes here, arbitrary, ranging from those which include most of the
built-up areas of the county that frames the census-defined "standard
metropolitan area," as is typical of the smaller metropolitan areas, to the
largest areas where the central cities typically enclose only a third to a
quarter of the total. Finely spun analyses of central city and suburban
shares of employment in various industries are almost invariably spe-
cious. It would be much more meaningful for most purposes to compare, over time and across diverse places, the changing share and composition of "core area" industry and population at some uniform, relative

point in space, such as half the distance from the center to the edge of the urban area, or some constant, absolute point, such as the ring enclosed by radii of half a mile and three miles out.)

Prediction, speculation, or hope that the service industry will come to the rescue of the central business district, and through it infuse new life into the inner city labor submarket, rests in large measure on a favorable trend in services. Increasing per capita income leads to more than proportionate increases in the consumption of *professional* services. Again, increasing pressures to conserve resources and to control pollution — to reduce physical inputs and outputs — should act to raise the price of goods relative to services and add a favorable price effect to the favorable income effect. A steadily rising share of total income spent on services combines with a relatively slow rate of increase in productivity per man-hour to almost ensure that the service industry will absorb a growing proportion of the national labor force.

If service workers receive wage increases similar to other workers, all keyed to the average increase in labor productivity, their below-average increase in productivity will cause service prices to rise relative to other prices. It seems reasonable to assume that in the near future, this adverse relative price effect will offset *in part* the favorable income effect but, as in the past, not by enough to prevent at least a slow, steady increase in the share of total income spent on services. Since even a constant proportion of expenditures would command a rising proportion of the labor force in a sector of below-average increase in labor productivity, there seems to be no place for service employment to go but up, and at a much faster than average rate of growth.

The simultaneous suburbanization of manufacturing and the middle-class white population served to separate black males from the main source of blue-collar work and place them at a competitive disadvantage in the labor market, but black females may well have benefited on net from postwar locational trends in the large metropolitan area. Because middle-class whites suburbanized faster and farther than *office* employment, the growing separation of white females from central business district offices has created growing shortages of clerical and secretarial labor in the inner city. Impressionistic reports indicate that Manhattan office managers, although pressed for clerical and secretarial help, have been slow to substitute black and Puerto Rican females for their traditional labor force. But increasingly, they are reluctantly accepting unfamiliar life-styles and are upgrading minority females.

The response to the current and growing shortage of semiskilled and skilled female white-collar labor in the inner city could, admittedly, prove in the long run to be unfavorable to minority workers if this greatly accelerates the relocation of offices to the suburbs, nearer the new communities of their traditional labor supply. A competitive advantage in residential location and work access would be turned into a competitive disadvantage if offices begin to move outward faster than minority group white-collar workers do. But this seems unlikely. Besides, the suburbanization of retail trade and office work does not create quite as difficult a public transportation problem as does the suburbanization of manufacturing. Stores and offices tend to cluster in ways that facilitate provision of mass transit service from the inner city, while manufacturing plants tend to be more dispersed, and even when they are contiguous, tend to sprawl over acreages so vast that any access except by automobile is difficult to arrange.

What is the net balance in the change in demand for sales, clerical, and paraprofessional labor, as experienced by minority group females, due to the suburban drift of both the relevant workplaces and the residences of majority group white females? Deductively, we would expect the net competitive position of inner city females to be improving in metropolitan areas that have strong "central place functions" and where old downtowns have retained most of their earlier vitality (New York City, Chicago, and San Francisco come to mind). Conversely, the larger manufacturing centers, such as Detroit, Cleveland, Milwaukee, and St. Louis, with weak regional roles and relatively small hinterlands, would seem to be hard pressed to prevent a net weakening in the competitive position of inner city female white-collar workers. While we do need more conceptual work here, we have an even greater need for a substantial amount of careful empirical work.

A step in this direction was taken in the Labor Department's report (October 1969) on selected variations in labor force participation, unemployment rates, occupational profiles, work experience, weekly earnings, annual family incomes, and educational levels in selected inner city areas of concentrated poverty in Atlanta, Chicago, Detroit, Houston, Los Angeles, and New York. However, this was but a simple descriptive piece which stopped far short of the point at which it might have illuminated the balance of forces in urban growth and development as they bear on the demand and supply for various kinds of labor in the inner city labor submarket.

MANUFACTURING IN THE CENTRAL CITY

Central city industrial development strategy will need to distinguish between the old and the new. We could place the highest priority on holding in place those industries already in hand. Have they not already demonstrated that they are at home and adjusted to their present location? But the past is not always prologue; the technology of the old industries of the central city may have changed, calling for new conditions, and the conditions of the central city itself have of course changed significantly.

It is no longer necessary to dwell at length on the now well-appreciated advantages of the suburbs for mass production. Only there can large vacant sites be found for stretched-out, one-floor assembly lines and the huge parking lots needed for the workers' automobiles. Rather than repeat familiar arguments, let us here add a less noticed advantage: Manufacturing may favor a suburban location because it is less dependent there on the presence of good local government — a most scarce resource. The high-density central city generates intense interactions and heavy "spillover costs," calling for a strong local public authority with a sure hand in mediation, coordination, and regulation. To the extent that local public policy and public management are not up to the task, plants find it much simpler to locate in the suburbs where government is not better and probably not as good, but the demands on it are so light that ineptness is more easily tolerated.

Activity is much more dispersed in the suburbs, therefore "neighborhood effects" (e.g., heavy truck traffic on residential streets, unsightly storage yards, noise, and smoke) are less troublesome, and the manufacturing plant owners feel a greater freedom of independent action. And looking ahead, one can see that the low-density land-use patterns of the suburbs afford a flexibility that permits easier adaptation to change; in the tightly built-up inner city, every move makes waves that create conflicts of interest and force bitter confrontations. (One of the more interesting suggestions for programming inner city land is that we use some of our large parks for new manufacturing plants that require large sites and that we replace the lost recreational space with smaller and closer, and perhaps safer, new parks on land released by residential clearance — housing abandonment [U.S. Department of Commerce, May 1970, p. 92].)

We have come to the time for the recycling of our cities: urban renewal, industrial redevelopment, large population relocations, and major transportation investments. This will not be a pleasant period in which to do business in the inner city, even with a strong and sophisticated local public sector in command. We have never been this way before, thus the uncertainties may be even more unsettling than the delays. Spreading out in the suburbs and paying the modest extra costs of transportation probably seem to be the cheapest way of doing business more often than not. The extra transportation cost of overcoming lower densities is usually less than the extra cost of moving through mismanaged higher densities — "congestion."

Are inner city industries engaged more than proportionately in the production of old products in old ways — production processes that have had time to become rationalized and routinized? Perhaps these invariably older, nearly obsolete plants employ simpler skills and thereby fill a crucial need in inner city labor markets. Or does inner city manufacturing tend more toward job shops that do custom work, or make short production runs on short notice, employing highly skilled or versatile labor?

The inner city has long been celebrated as the leading edge of the manufacturing economy of the metropolitan area and therefore of the nation. The Vernon–Hoover study of the New York City economy made much of the inner city "lofts" as being the hothouses of invention and innovation. New small businesses, pressed to use the lowest rent workspace and forced by a paucity of staff to draw heavily on outside professional and technical consultants, settled for older buildings in the inner city near the center of expertise and skill. Even if the old lofts did serve in the past to incubate new firms and new industries — and remarkably little study has followed the original New York findings, especially considering both the importance of that hypothesis and its wide currency in the profession — is this still true today? What has been the impact of the institutionalization of research and development within the large corporation and of the rise of the publicly subsidized research park? It is hard to ignore the serious deterioration of inner city buildings and central city public services, and the flight of skilled labor to distant residential areas, in reassessing this thesis.

Where is the cheap "loft space" of the 1970s, and where will it be in the 1980s? Reflection reminds one that the first postwar wave of industrial construction was in the first ring of suburbs, and simple arithmetic reminds one that these plants are now twenty years old. As the original owners begin to relocate in newer plants that are more appropriate to the new technologies of their industries, a large new supply of good used workspace becomes available, at reduced prices and rents, and is highly accessible to the suburban residences of skilled labor and the new suburban offices of key consultants.

Perhaps it was the availability of key talent and skill at the old downtown transportation hub (European immigrants?) as much or more than the cheap loft space that spawned industrial innovation in the inner city. Is the second generation of these entrepreneurs — small business inventors and innovators — a generation of suburban homeowners, typically 35-year-old heads of families with school-age children who find overwhelming convenience in locating their businesses near their homes? Are the new "lofts" in the old suburbs?

The inner city industrial development strategists might well be ambivalent as to which set of jobs they would prefer. Routine work and old industries cut current welfare rolls more because unskilled older workers are unlikely to seek and hold any but nearby jobs. But massing low-skill, low-wage, dead-end work does not build a strong community or an effective local public sector, and cannot therefore serve the long-run interests of the young. If the challenge is to mix routine old and demanding new activities in the inner city, the response would seem to lie more in blending old and new services than in recapturing manufacturing plants to become once again the cutting edge in applied science and engineering.

One could perhaps take the position that the role of the inner city manufacturing sector is instead to prepare nearby residents for eventual employment in the mainstream manufacturing economy building up in the suburbs — "graduation" to the suburbs in both work and home. In this view, a high rate of labor turnover is not only acceptable, it is a mark of success. Those manufacturing plants most appropriate for inner city sites would then be ones which provide a high proportion of entry jobs, a good beginning toward the development of skills, work discipline, and middle-class values and aspirations. Figuratively, these manufacturing plants would be extensions of the vocational high school — "finishing schools" for the working class.

Do we see the inner city manufacturing sector becoming increasingly a place where native-born slum dwellers and raw recruits from farms and small towns are processed — acculturated — into factory-trained and -disciplined emigrants to blue-collar suburbs and industrial satellites in that same or other metropolitan areas? Probably the most common concept of the inner city, and the most popular rationalization today of its decline, is that it has served as a kind of Ellis Island through which in-migrants pass as they move upward in socioeconomic status and outward in residence (Sternlieb, 1971; Long, 1971). The "concentric zone theory" of residential form implies such a pattern of movement in space, if we do indeed have an open society to any significant degree. But there has been remarkably little thought, or at least comment, on whether we do or should have a parallel concentric-zone hierarchy of workplaces.

The City as an Aging Stock of Capital

Different depreciation periods disrupt the locational linkages between different kinds of complementary capital. Factories typically become technically obsolete — even if not physically deteriorated — at least for their original purpose, in time periods much shorter than the useful life of workers' houses. Moreover, manufacturing plants are more specialized and do not filter down to lower income users as well as do houses. Besides, there are relatively few "poor" businesses looking for used plants; when firms fail, unlike households, they disappear. Thus plants that are close to workers' homes for the first thirty years of the life of the houses are abandoned and the jobs transferred to new plants much farther away for the entire latter half of the life of these houses. We come then to face the increasingly familiar problem of long and costly commuting for those who are least mobile and least able to afford it: the lower skill workers who have come late into possession of the older housing.

We have become increasingly aware of how important manufacturing jobs are to uneducated but able-bodied and highly motivated males, especially with the decline of employment in agriculture and the other extractive industries that long have been their mainstay. The free market fails to arrange the necessary realignments of home and the workplace automatically and alertly, in large part because the cost to private enterprise of adjusting to a shortage of unskilled workers is much less than the cost to society of their chronic unemployment. Machines can be substituted for hard-to-get and far away unskilled labor, getting the private employer off the hook.

But let us look ahead: Will the plants built in the new suburbs of 1945 to 1955 still be operating by the time the working poor blacks of the central city have finally "filtered up" and outward into nearby houses in 1980 and 1990? That is, will the low-skill black worker finally make it to the near suburbs about the time that manufacturing picks up and moves again to, say, a distant industrial satellite? We may in fact, as a matter of social policy, push factories out there to protect the quality of the *natural* environment — the deterioration of the social environment notwithstanding.

Again, will today's inner city population have drifted out to the older suburbs just about the time that the old downtowns have turned the corner and have become strongly resurgent as the sites of the new high services — the next round of "good jobs"? Office buildings do in fact obsolesce more slowly than manufacturing plants, and central business districts have shown more staying power than have central city industrial districts. Simply said, in 1990, with downtown flourishing again and the best manufacturing jobs in the new "clean" plants thirty to fifty miles out, the old, first-round suburbs, open then to all, could then be neither here nor there.

Certainly it would be most difficult to align, in time and space, factory construction and low-income house building, simply because we do not build houses for the poor, except in trivial amounts. They live overwhelmingly in old houses. We would need to phase in *current* factory construction with upper middle-income housing constructed thirty years *earlier* if low-skill, low-income workers are to be near the newer blue-collar workplaces for, say, two decades to come. Maybe we would benefit in the long run if plants indulged in "leapfrog sprawl" at the urban fringe, assuming that other new workplaces could come by in a decade or two and fill in the vacant sites — zoned industrial and held open. Can we learn to "time zone" land for industrial use at a future date? Is there a logical industrial component in a program of federally assisted state land banking?

It would be misleading to leave the impression that we now possess the knowledge and skills to plan and program land and capital so that aging plants and houses are juxtaposed in symbiotic patterns. Ideally perhaps, a given site would be first a place of high-skill operations near the new houses of upper middle-income families, the first owners; later a lower skill operation, more compatible with the second owners of that housing, would command that site. Perhaps the same plant shell could serve a number of successively simpler industrial operations. We know from casual observation that industrial plants do filter down from higher to lower uses — more profitable to less profitable firms — but we do not know nearly enough to provide the sound base that would justify the "social engineering" suggested here.

A physically much simpler but socially more radical home-workplace pattern or strategy would be to mix houses of diverse ages, sizes, and quality so that workers of all levels of skill and income could live in every labor submarket. This of course is a variation on the theme of residential mixing but at somewhat coarser grain and in somewhat more dynamic context than that in which it is usually offered for consideration.

This is a variation on the Lessinger (August 1962) argument for leapfrog "scatterization": Only small numbers of houses would be built at any given time on any given site, and be well separated from other subdivisions of that age housing. When the gaps fill in later, a building pattern of mixed ages and replacement dates is created. Because the buildings will tend to wear out and be replaced piecemeal, the renewal of the area will be constant and gradual, in striking contrast to the concentrated and simultaneous aging, blight, and demolition that inevitably follow sixty or seventy years after a wave of massed new construction. Social mixing of course is likely to be every bit as difficult to achieve politically as synchronized residential-nonresidential filtering would be to achieve physically.

Toward a Hierarchy of Labor Submarkets

An all-out effort to improve transportation over the full reaches of the large and enlarging metropolitan area could perhaps preserve it as a unified labor market. But this position could also be seen as a policy of maximizing movement and one probably committing the local public economy to a substantial subsidization of movement. Such a position would seem to clash with our mounting concern for the quality of the urban environment (e.g., air pollution) and the deepening energy crisis.

Pressures are already building up, especially in the older metropolises where congestion and pollution are worse and the transportation alternatives are better (e.g., a legacy of arterial railroads as in Chicago), to implement a system of heavy user charges on automobile movement designed to force householders to economize on miles traveled by private vehicle. In the long run, such action could well bring into being a high-quality and nearly ubiquitous public transportation system, but the construction period would be at least a full decade, and probably closer to two decades. During the transitional stage, in response to the high money cost of commuting by automobile or the high time cost of using the still inadequate public transit system, a considerable number of skilled and affluent workers would probably "choose" to move their homes nearer their workplaces (and some have the power to move their workplaces nearer their homes). On the average, a fifth of the households do move every year.

Even in the long run, with good public transit systems, the conservation of energy and the protection of the natural environment suggest forcing a shortening of trips, additionally subdividing the local labor market, at least until that distant day, if ever, when public transportation is so efficient and so protective of the environment that we feel we can afford to permit if not encourage long journeys to work — heavy cross-commuting. For the low-wage worker, dependent on public transportation, access to a *distant* workplace seems likely to get worse before it gets better.

Even public transportation consumes appreciable amounts of energy, thus perhaps only those workers with the scarcest talents will be encouraged to range back and forth across the full reaches of the largest metropolitan area, treating it as the single, indivisible, local labor market that we so blithely assume it to be. Rising social costs of movement would then be reflected in rising user charges and would induce shorter trips to work with each step downward in skill and income (i.e., would induce one to live near one's work). Metropolitan area labor markets could come to be, even more than now, a hierarchy of commuting spaces, broadening with the scarcity and the value of the skill. Only high-skill, high-income workers could afford to pay daily the high tolls or fares of long trips.

If so, what would come to be most crucial is a wide dispersion of low-income housing, with all four quadrants of the local labor market balanced in housing and able to accommodate the least mobile. We might come to see three or four or more easily distinguishable, even if slightly overlapping, low-skill labor submarkets spread round the urban region. The less skilled retail trade and personal service workers, to avoid long automobile trips at high money cost or long transit trips at high time cost, would come to live clustered round each large suburban shopping center — each new "uptown."

CENTERS AND RINGS

It has already become inexcusably naïve among urbanists to speak of *the* central city and *the* suburbs. Large metropolitan areas can increasingly be described as a loose federation of a small number of centers and surrounding rings — "suburbs" that process materials and produce goods ringing "central cities" that process information and deliver services. The dualism in these complex local economies, referred to earlier, is itself pluralistic in that the various central cities are typically specialized, as in finance, law, and government (e.g., the old downtown), or higher education (e.g., "university city"), or recreation, and also in the fact that some are "more equal" than others (e.g., the old downtown). So, too, do the different manufacturing-residential rings vary in occupational and demographic composition.

What most of these centers have in common is a strong retail trade base, often tracing their very origins back to trade. A major regional shopping center must draw on and in turn draws together about a quarter of a million persons, and tends to become at least a thin downtown to that population, as it adds a few restaurants and theaters to its mall. In the course of generating a wide range of retail trade and personal service jobs, the comparative shopping center and its satellites become a principal source of the entry and part-time jobs that are so crucial to the employment of the youth, the elderly, the handicapped, and the housewife. Moreover, if we were to reinforce these many centers with community colleges and other facilities for continuing education, we have much of the social overhead needed for a strong, balanced, and progressive labor submarket. It would seem to be almost essential that we make provision for strong programs in manpower training and higher education in these new "downtowns," if we see them as hubs of our local submarkets, and especially if we tolerate dropping out of "irrelevant" high schools (see chapter 6 for further discussion on this topic) or turn from compulsive full-time college education or graduation from high school to lifelong, part-time "continuing education."

The many subeconomies and labor submarkets of the very large metropolitan area may come to be bound together by at least two distinct long-distance movements:

(1) Long journeys to work of the most skilled workers and scarcest talents (e.g., professional workers and managers)

(2) The once- or twice-a-week trips to theaters, museums, and sports stadiums, and for advanced study (conferences?)

Perhaps somewhere in this evolving system of centers and rings we can find the means to provide:

(1) The great urban scale that the affluent professional seeks

(2) The small city sense of community that (pollsters tell us) the blue-collar worker seeks

(3) All within a deep sense of appreciation for and protection of the natural environment

Perhaps big cities do have the potential to be "all things to all men," but only if we become much better designers and builders.

REFERENCES

Lessinger, Jack. "The Case for Scatterization." *Journal of the American Institute of Planners* (August 1962).

Long, Norton E. "The City as Reservation." *The Public Interest* (Fall 1971).

Sternlieb, George. "The City as Sandbox." *The Public Interest* (Fall 1971).

Thompson, Wilbur R. "Internal and External Factors in the Development of Urban Economies." In *Issues in Urban Economics.* Edited by Harvey S. Perloff and Lowdon Wingo, Jr. Baltimore: The Johns Hopkins Press. 1968.

U.S. Department of Commerce, Economic Development Administration, Mayors' Conference for Economic and Cultural Development. *A Partnership for Action: Mid-Chicago Economic Development Project.* Washington, D.C.: U.S. Government Printing Office. May 1970.

U.S. Department of Labor, Bureau of Labor Statistics. *Employment Situation in Poverty Areas of Six Cities, July 1968–June 1969.* Report no. 370. Washington, D.C.: U.S. Government Printing Office. October 1969.

2
Social and Demographic Trends: Focus on Race

KARL E. TAEUBER*

The changing demographic, social, and economic contours of the American metropolis in the 1950s and 1960s are a matter of common information. Recent public debate has focused on the plight of the central cities vs the suburbs. In exaggerated but sharp focus, central cities have been seen as losing all manner of good things to the suburbs and keeping or attracting all manner of bad things. Among the "good" things increasingly being found in the suburbs are jobs, especially in newer industries, property with a high value for taxation purposes, middle- and high-income consumers, and young white families. Among the "bad" things perceived as concentrating in the central cities are old, deteriorating housing, an outmoded physical plant, black people of all ages, the welfare population, inadequate and corrupt municipal services, pollution, congestion, crime, and many other social problems. This widely shared perspective, albeit in more sophisticated language, underlies most other current discussions of the changing metropolis. A decade ago the focus would have been on the metropolis as an entity — on its expansion into an all-consuming megapolitan system that seemed to spell the ruination of our rural and agricultural territory, or perhaps on the severe plight of the occasional metropolis left behind by the forces

* Professor of sociology and fellow, Institute for Research on Poverty, University of Wisconsin. The research reported here was supported in part by funds granted to the Institute by the Office of Economic Opportunity. The conclusions and interpretations are the sole responsibility of the author.

of industrial expansion and economic growth. There is no rule against academicians drifting with the tides of public debate. The internal structure of the contemporary metropolis provides more than ample material for demographic assessment and discussion.

Demographers have a penchant for mining the data of the last census and hence for consistently being out of date. To the managers and politicians, lack of timeliness tends to characterize even those of us who pore over the latest Current Population Survey results issued only one or two years ago. Demographers have many techniques for looking into the future, but because of their repeated bitter experience with precise prognostication, they are in general less willing than almost any other species of social analyst to engage in foretelling the future. I have no greater prevision than the rest of my colleagues. We all have difficulty seeing fundamental social change even when it is far advanced. The new dynamics of the changing metropolis of the 1970s will only become obvious a few years from now when we can look back. With no further apology, I draw heavily in my assessment of the 1970s on a summary and interpretation of the 1960s.

The general volume of the 1960 Census Monograph series includes a 41-page chapter on urbanization, a 67-page chapter on metropolitan dynamics, three separate chapters on population redistribution and migration, and still more chapters on major social and economic characteristics and trends in fertility and mortality. There would be little point in my trying in the short space available to update such a mass of information or to review all other relevant data documenting and challenging the general proposition that central cities have been on the short end of the stick. Besides, the most relevant manpower aspects are reviewed by Wilbur Thompson and several other authors.

My special interest is demographic aspects of race relations in the contemporary United States. I shall narrow the focus by using this topic to illustrate certain themes that warrant emphasis. A technical reason for concentrating on the racial aspects of metropolitan structure is that race is among the complete-count census items rather than the sample items, and hence the data on race were tabulated earlier and have been available longer than most of the data on social and economic attributes. A further and compelling reason for a focus on race is that the playing out of the civil rights movement of the late 1950s and early 1960s and the urban violence of the late 1960s have colored all subsequent discussions of the changing character of the metropolis.

By the time the civil rights movement was in full swing, trying to transform race relations in the traditional deep South, the black population of the United States was already more urbanized and more metropolitanized than the white population. At the time of the 1970 census, 71 percent of the black population lived in metropolitan areas, as compared to 64 percent of the white population. The central cities of our metropolitan areas were home for more than half (55 percent) of the nation's blacks, as compared to a fourth of whites. The portion of the metropolitan areas outside the central cities (i.e., the suburbs) contained 16 percent of blacks, as compared to 39 percent of the nation's whites.

Major population transformations tend to work themselves out over a considerable period of time. The concentration of black population in central cities has been a continuing process throughout this century and has been a particularly rapid process during the last three decades. During the early decades of this century, the white central city population was also increasing rapidly. In recent decades, the white increase slowed to a trickle and in many individual metropolitan areas turned into a major decrease. The percentage that blacks compose of the total central city population increased slowly in the early decades and more rapidly in recent decades. The central city proportion of blacks was about 6.5 percent in 1900, 7 percent in 1920, and 10 percent in 1940. The last three census figures showed 12 percent for 1950, 17 percent for 1960, and 21.5 percent for 1970.

The so-called "blackening" of the central cities is not a new process, nor is "whitening" of the suburbs. The proportion that blacks composed of the suburban population in 1900 was 9 percent. Blacks did not participate to any great degree in the rapid suburbanization of the 1910s and 1920s, and the proportion of blacks dropped to about 5 percent in 1940. It has remained near that figure at each subsequent census.

At various times since the mid-1950s there have been commentators who see some evidence of the beginning of a new era of black suburbanization. The fact that black suburban population increased nearly as rapidly during the last thirty years as did the white suburban population could be taken to indicate that such a new era already exists. True enough; but two cautions are in order. The first is that black participation in suburbanization is still a very small phenomenon numerically in comparison to the large numbers involved in the white population. In 1900 there were already a million blacks living outside central cities — many were living in enclaves or small towns that happened to fall within the metropolitan boundaries established at midcentury. By 1970 this figure had increased to 3.6 million. For whites the growth was from 11 million in 1900 to more than 70 million in 1970.

A second point flows from the fact that my definition of suburbanization is an elementary statistical one and does not convey any necessary concomitant social overlay. By black suburbanization I simply mean an increase in black population outside central cities but within the limits of metropolitan areas. This statistical approach does not entail notions of "suburbanization as a way of life." Nor does black suburbanization necessarily entail residential integration; indeed there is evidence it does not. Consider for example the Chicago metropolitan area. From 1950 to 1970 the black population in the Chicago suburbs increased from 43,600 to 128,300. Of the total increase of 85,000 blacks, two-thirds went to nine older suburbs that include much industry within their boundaries and contain predominantly old housing, much of it rental units. Another fourth of the black suburban increase went to five small residential suburbs that are almost entirely black or that contain predominantly black residential areas. The rest of Chicago's suburbs are home for more than three million whites but added fewer than ten thousand black residents during the twenty-year period.

In several metropolitan regions black residential areas have for many years reached to the city limits but until recently had not crossed them. Very high percentage increases in black suburban population are now occurring in some of these places. The number of blacks in the suburbs of Cleveland increased by 453 percent from 1960 to 1970, from 8,000 to 45,000 persons. A 98 percent increase in the Washington area's suburban black population represented an increase from 84,000 to 166,000 persons. A 55 percent increase in the black suburban population of the New York metropolitan area occurred because of an increase in the numbers from 140,000 to 217,000. One who sees this as the wave of the future must make a wild (albeit possibly correct) forecast. We may indeed be witnessing in these areas the beginning of a major new trend, but the numbers involved are impressive only in contrast to the smaller numbers of suburban blacks previously.

To return the focus on black population to the central cities, let me cite aggregate national change data for cities and suburbs. The white suburban population increased during the last decade by fifteen million persons. The black suburban population increased by 832,000 persons. In central cities there was a decline in white population of 607,000 persons and a black increase of more than three million persons.

Our awareness of the racial composition of central cities has been colored in recent years by the considerable attention given to cities such as Newark and the District of Columbia, where blacks have become a majority. The recent election of black mayors in Atlanta and Los Angeles contributes to an impression that blacks are "taking over" in increasingly more cities. Is this truly the wave of the future? Are the dynamics of population change pushing us inexorably toward an increasing geographic and political apartheid? I shall attempt two answers: the first in terms of the national aggregate, the other in terms of diversity among metropolitan areas. Both answers will be embarrassingly equivocal.

First, I shall consider trends at the national level. Any process of rapid demographic change tends to alter the structural circumstances that gave rise to the process, even apart from changes in the underlying social and economic phenomena. The transformation of the United States from a rural to a metropolitan nation has already occurred. The nonmetropolitan population that was the source of much of the increase in metropolitan population has become an ever smaller proportion of the total population. Migration from nonmetropolitan areas, even if it continues at the same rates as in the past, will produce a much slower rate of increment to the metropolitan numbers.

The aggregate rate of metropolitan growth is a variable that depends not only on the rate at which nonmetropolitan areas contribute people to metropolitan areas, but also on the rate of natural increase and on the rate of net immigration from abroad. Immigration is controlled by law and is ordinarily projected at a relatively constant low level. Fertility in recent years has dropped far below almost everyone's projections and has led to marked revisions in the government's projections of growth of the national population. In the mid-1960s considerable attention was given to the need to devise new methods for accommodating the rapid population growth foreseen for the United States by the turn of the century. The most common round number was that the nation would add a hundred million people by the year 2000 and that virtually all of this increase would go to metropolitan areas. Now we have projections at least equally reasonable that indicate the metropolitan increment may be less than half that number.

The assumption that metropolitan areas will capture virtually all of the population growth of the nation during the next three decades has become subject to question and interpretation. Part of the process of metropolitan growth is artifactual — as small cities grow beyond the fifty thousand population mark, the Office of Management and Budget designates additional metropolitan areas, and as larger areas spread out, additional counties are incorporated into the metropolitan category. In many of these cases there has been no sudden change in the social, economic, and territorial organization of society. In addition, the current concept of metropolitan areas may become an increasingly inadequate means for describing the territorial distribution of population. Just as the long-used concepts of rural farm, rural nonfarm, and urban place have lost utility, so may the standard metropolitan statistical area (SMSA) become inadequate for assessing future trends. Between 1960 and 1970 the nonmetropolitan population grew faster than the metropolitan population in New York, New Jersey, and most of the New England states. Throughout our history this northeastern part of the nation has led the rest in the fundamental patterns of population redistribution — in initial agricultural settlement, in urbanization and diminished rural densities, in the formation of metropolitan complexes, and now, perhaps, in the spread of settlement patterns beyond the domain of the metropolis. The new megalopolis, if such it is, cannot be simply an expanded metropolis or a proliferation of metropoles. If the rest of the nation is about to embark on a new era of greater balance between rates of nonmetropolitan and metropolitan growth, as well as slower rates in each, then the dynamics of differential central city and suburban growth will also be altered.

Suppose the pattern of the 1950s and 1960s does continue unaltered in the 1970s. Shall we expect a large number of cities to achieve black majorities? Consider the tally in Table 1, derived from a table listing

TABLE 1

Distribution of Central Cities by Proportion of Blacks
(1970)

Rank Order of Cities	Less than 30%	30 to 39.9%	40 to 49.9%	50% and Over
Top fifty	36	6	5	3
Second fifty	41	6	3	
Bottom 143	126	13	4	

SOURCE: Bureau of the Census, U.S. Department of Commerce, *Census of Population, 1970* (Washington, D.C.: U.S. Government Printing Office, 1971).

all 243 metropolitan areas in rank order by size (U.S. Department of Commerce, 1971). The tally shows the number of areas in which the central city has the specified percentage of blacks. The three central cities with a black majority were the District of Columbia, Newark, and Atlanta. (In this tally, Gary is merged with Hammond and East Chicago, Indiana, and the combined central cities do not approach a black majority.)

Among the twelve cities with a black percentage of between 40 and 50, most had sharp increases in that percentage during the decade of the 1960s, but a few did not: From 1960 to 1970 the percentage in Birmingham and Pine Bluff increased from 40 to 42, that in Richmond remained steady at 42, and that in Charleston, South Carolina, declined from 51 to 45. The likeliest candidates for early entry into the black majority ranks are the remaining eight cities which in 1970 had more than 40 percent blacks: Atlantic City, Augusta, Baltimore, Detroit, New Orleans, Savannah, St. Louis, and Wilmington.

Among the 25 cities with black percentages between 30 and 40, there is a number of southern cities in which the percentage has recently declined, remained stable, or increased only slowly. Some of these southern cities are still growing and attracting additional white population; many are still experiencing black outmigration to northern cities and larger southern cities. A few of the cities with black percentages between 30 and 40 might possibly reach black majority ranks by 1980. Altogether then, if the past trends continue, about twelve of the 243 metropolitan areas may by 1980 have black majorities in their central cities.

It may seem paradoxical that continued rapid "blackening" of the nation's central cities is likely to leave us in 1980 with 95 percent of those cities having white population in the majority. The paradox is easily resolved if it is remembered that blacks are a small minority of the total population. There simply are not enough blacks in the country for them to form majorities in every central city. A few numbers taken from the 1970 census are shown in Table 2. If all of the nonmetropolitan black population moved immediately to the central cities and half of the white population in the central cities moved out, whites would still form a majority of the nation's central city population.

Certain aspects of the demographic dynamics of the three decades from 1940 to 1970 cannot be repeated. The 1970s were a period of winding down of the pattern established during those three decades, mingled

TABLE 2

Distribution of Blacks and Whites in Various Areas
(1970)

Type of Area	Population (millions)		Percentage of Blacks
	Blacks	Whites	
Central cities	12.6	45.1	21.8%
Suburbs	3.5	68.5	4.9
Nonmetropolitan	6.7	63.8	9.5

SOURCE: Bureau of the Census, U.S. Department of Commerce, *Census of Population, 1970* (Washington, D.C.: U.S. Government Printing Office, 1971).

with the emergence of a new pattern whose shape is not yet clear. One must equivocate concerning the dynamics of the 1970s and the situation we may expect to reach by 1980. Perhaps later scholars will tack the 1970s onto the 1940s through 1960s as the period of large-scale black urbanization and northward movement, concentrated in central city residential areas previously occupied by whites who were in a phase of rapid outward movement from central cities. But I think this pattern is largely played out and will diminish in intensity during this decade. In 1940, 55 percent of the black population lived outside metropolitan areas, and 77 percent lived in the South. Even in 1960, two-thirds of southern blacks lived outside metropolitan areas. Today a majority of the black population lives outside the South; but even in the South a majority of the blacks is already metropolitan based.

Let us look at an even longer period of time: from 1910 to 1970. During those years the black population of the United States more than doubled. The black population in Alabama, Arkansas, Kentucky, Mississippi, and South Carolina declined. The black population in Georgia and West Virginia grew less than 10 percent. The great migrations of those six decades transferred to a few large cities in the northern and border states large numbers of young blacks who have become the parents of succeeding generations. The natural increase of the black population now occurs largely within cities. Migration of blacks from the rural South and from many of the smaller southern cities may be expected to continue, but the rural and nonmetropolitan migrants seeking a better life are no longer the dominant force in black population growth and redistribution.

Each mass migration has its own internal dynamic, first of self-reinforcement and later of self-limitation. In the early phases, expansion of channels of communication and flow of information tend to accelerate the movement. The black exodus from the rural South was led by youth. As they reached adulthood, they sought new opportunities. Nearly all of the young blacks reaching age fifteen to twenty in the rural South during the last six decades have moved elsewhere in search of opportunity. Many went to a nearby city, while others migrated to larger cities in the South or North. Meanwhile, many young blacks growing up in the smaller cities of the South also moved to larger cities of the North and South, and so on in a great sequence of migrations.

Each wave of young migrants quickly reached the family formation stage and produced a new generation of young blacks growing up in the new locations. In this way, large-scale migration transfers the natural increase from the places of origin to the places of destination. The current generation of black youth is largely a product of the metropolitan system, and it is unlikely that their patterns of residential redistribution will resemble the patterns established by their parents and grandparents of moving in ever-greater numbers to a small number of cities with huge black populations.

The dynamics of black population redistribution are subject to shifts simply as a result of the long-sustained character of the black "great migrations." But the general redistribution trends of the 1940s and 1950s continued strong through the 1960s. How quickly they will abate in the 1970s (and 1980s) remains to be seen. There are several reasons to expect a fairly rapid shift.

The process of population redistribution during the last 25 years was accelerated by the baby boom which produced ever-increasing numbers of youth in the migration-prone ages. We are entering a period where these numbers are relatively stable and in a few more years are slated to decline. Increasing numbers and proportions of urban blacks are obtaining jobs with considerable employment security and with income levels that place them in the middle-income brackets, or what may be referred to as the income brackets where home ownership is a distinct possibility.

Several studies of urban housing patterns have shown that although blacks are highly segregated, similar patterns operate within the black as within the white housing market. That is, persons who are economically better off are continually seeking improved housing by moving farther away from the center of the city or from the center of older and more densely settled residential areas. In many social and economic trends, blacks have followed somewhat the same pattern as whites, but with a gap of ten, twenty, or thirty years. It is at least plausible that this may be the case for home ownership and metropolitan decentralization. Supportive evidence is provided in data on recent black migration to some of the northern cities with large black populations.

Between 1960 and 1970 there was a net migration of blacks *from* Cincinnati, Cleveland, Pittsburgh, and St. Louis. Net migration *to* Philadelphia and Gary–Hammond–East Chicago (and also to Baltimore and Washington) was less than 10 percent during the decade. To date, not much of the black outmigration is to the suburbs — rather it seems to flow to cities with smaller black populations — but the indications of a reduced migratory influx to the traditional destinations of black migrants may portend more extensive changes in the 1970s.

In a period of slower black population increase, there is increased possibility for fairly rapid decline in residential segregation, if the process can ever get fully started. Were there to be a fair scattering of blacks throughout a metropolitan area, the process could easily accelerate. As more areas open to blacks, the process of rapid expansion of blacks into individual, narrowly circumscribed areas would diminish. At the same time the possibility for whites to escape completely having blacks as neighbors would be diminished. The perception that any neighborhood containing some blacks is en route to becoming solidly black would lose much of its validity.

But let us take a closer look at the desegregation issue. Patterns of residential segregation seem to be among the most tenacious of the many forms of racial segregation. Legal efforts to counteract racial discrimination in the housing market are still in their infancy and are not being vigorously pursued by federal authorities or by many state and local agencies. The nation has had difficulty in producing as many new housing starts as various commissions and plans have indicated are necessary, both to house new households and to provide for a modest level of replacement of existing stock. The white population is also experiencing increasing economic status and is more able than the black population to afford the newest suburban housing. High interest rates and rapidly inflating costs of new housing are limiting this market, and thus may slow down the entire filtering process through which additional vacancies are supposed to occur at all housing price levels.

There will be a continuing strong demand on the part of the black population for additional and more desirable housing within metropolitan areas. Fifty-four percent of central city blacks live in housing that was built before 1940. Because there was little construction of new housing throughout the nation during the 1930s, most of the pre-1940 housing is indeed old. To be sure, 47 percent of the white population in central cities also live in housing built before 1940. And whites in 1970 occupied four times as many such units as did blacks. Central cities are likely to continue to experience considerable outmigration from areas of older housing, and blacks as well as whites will be active in the search for better housing.

There are two kinds of answers to the question of the future rate of "blackening" of our central cities. The first is concentrated on national trends; the second focuses on the diversity among metropolitan areas. Discussions of migration trends and of variation among areas in the percentage that blacks comprise central city populations have already touched on this aspect. The nation's 243 metropolitan areas are not all alike; some are farther along in certain trends than others. But the point to make is stronger than these assertions of ordinary variation round the mean. There are some simple tabulations that demonstrate an enormous diversity of process — of population dynamics — as well as of current structure and rates of change. James Tirone, in his management view of labor force research in chapter 5, has called for attention to local labor markets in their full complexity. By proceeding from national aggregate data to data for more than two hundred separate metropolitan areas, the present chapter takes a small step in this direction.

The tables that follow are designed to display aspects of the diversity in racial population dynamics among the nation's metropolitan areas. They are tallies of the number of areas that experienced specified patterns of change. For three of the four tables, the universe is 217 metropolitan areas, each with a population in 1970 of a hundred thousand inhabitants or more. (The 26 officially designated metropolitan areas of less than this number are omitted from the tallies.) For the third table in this sequence, the universe is restricted to the 65 metropolitan areas of at least five hundred thousand population, simply because the Census Bureau was unable to prepare suitable net migration estimates by race for many of the smaller areas. Even for some of the large areas, the estimates are admittedly made from an inadequate data base. All of the data in the tables pertaining to 1960 use the 1970 census definitions of metropolitan area boundaries. The city-suburb distinction is based upon the central city boundaries at each census date. For certain analyses of change, it is essential to adjust 1970 data to reflect population within the 1960 boundaries. No such adjustment was made with these data, and hence annexation is one factor augmenting some of the cited central city growth rates and slowing down some of the cited suburban growth rates.

Panels A and B of Table 3 document changes between 1960 and 1970 in the percentage that blacks compose of the central city populations. In both South and North, about two-thirds of the metropolitan areas remained within the same 10 percentage point range in 1970 as in 1960. In the North, all of the areas that shifted categories moved into a higher percentage of blacks. Indeed most of the areas that started the decade with a central city population more than 10 percent black had shifted to a higher percentage of blacks by 1970. The main stability was for the eighty areas that were less than 10 percent black in 1960. In the South, some areas shifted categories into a lower percentage of blacks, although shifting to a higher percentage was more frequent.

Panels C and D of the table show the quite restricted degree of change in suburban percentages black. In the South, two-thirds of metropolitan areas again are found on the main diagonal, representing no shift in categories, but all areas that shifted moved in the direction of reduced percentages black. In the North, the suburbs were in 1960 and remained in 1970 a white preserve.

An increase in percentage black can arise from a decrease in white population and an increase in black population, or from a more rapid white than black decrease, or from a more rapid black than white increase. A decrease in percentage black can similarly be categorized into three distinct patterns. The tally in Table 4 compares the black and white changes in central city populations, 1960 to 1970. Only twelve areas experienced central city losses of both black and white population. Another 86 areas lost white central city population but gained blacks; the rate of black gains varied enormously.

Of the areas that gained central city whites, seven had a loss of blacks and at least twelve more had a lower rate of gain of blacks than of whites and hence had a decrease in percentage black. The remaining 105 areas in which both white and black population increased are spread among the full range of categories presented. The common pattern displayed in Table 3 of increasing percentage of blacks in central cities is seen from

TABLE 3

Black Population as a Percentage of Total Population,
for Central Cities and Suburbs*
(1970 compared to 1960)

1960	1970					
	0 to 10%	10 to 20%	20 to 30%	30 to 40%	40 to 50%	50% or More
A. Central cities (South)						
0 to 10%	12	3				
10 to 20%	1	11	2			
20 to 30%		2	16	5	1	
30 to 40%			2	11	4	1
40 to 50%				2	2	
50% or more					1	1
B. Central cities (North and West)						
0 to 10%	82	24				
10 to 20%		10	12	1		
20 to 30%			1	6	2	
30 to 40%					1	1
40 to 50%						
50% or more						
C. Suburbs (South)						
0 to 10%	32					
10 to 20%	4	10				
20 to 30%		13	8			
30 to 40%			4	2		
40 to 50%				3		
50% or more						
D. Suburbs (North and West)						
0 to 10%	139					
10 to 20%						
20 to 30%						
30 to 40%						
40 to 50%						
50% or more						

* Figures in the table are numbers of metropolitan areas. Tally includes all metropolitan areas having a total population in 1970 greater than a hundred thousand — 140 areas in the North and West and 77 in the South. For Jacksonville, Florida, the central city is coextensive with the metropolitan area, and there are no suburbs.

TABLE 4

Change in Central City Population,
Blacks Compared to Whites*
(1960 to 1970)

Change in White Population		Change in Black Population					
		Percent Gain					
	Loss	0 to 10%	10 to 20%	20 to 30%	30 to 40%	40 to 50%	50% or More
Percent loss:							
−20% or less 3	1	2	1	5	1	3
−10 to −20% 4	4	5	6	8	1	6
0 to −10% 5	7	14	3	2	4	15
Percent gain:							
0 to +10% 3	4	2	3	7	2	10
+10 to +20% 4	3	7	3	5	3	17
+20% or more	2	7	4	4	3	24

* Figures in the table are numbers of central cities. Tally includes all 217 metropolitan areas having a total population in 1970 greater than a hundred thousand.

the evidence in Table 4 to have arisen from a great diversity among areas in direction and magnitude of change in white and black populations.

Change in a central city's white or black population arises from natural increase (births minus deaths) and net migration (in-migration minus outmigration), and in some cases from territorial annexation. There is marked variation among cities in rates of natural increase. The central cities of Tampa and St. Petersburg had a loss from natural increase of 1.2 percent in their white population between 1960 and 1970; Anaheim, Garden Grove, and Santa Ana, California, had a white natural increase of 23 percent. Areal variation in rates of natural increase arises in only small part from variation in age-specific fertility and mortality rates. In much larger part, it arises from areal variation in age composition and in the rate of net migration. High rates of migration early in the decade add or subtract families in the reproductive ages and otherwise alter the age structure. Rates of net migration are somewhat varied. From 1960 to 1970, Las Vegas had a white population gain from net migration of 76 percent; Washington, D.C., had a loss of 40 percent.

Migration rates for a ten-year period must be estimated, and the appropriate estimates separately for blacks and whites have not been made for all metropolitan areas. In Table 5, central city net migration rates for blacks are compared to those for whites for sixty of the 65 largest metropolitan areas. Even with the broad categories used for the tally, there is evidently a diversity of metropolitan experiences and little relationship between rates of white migration and rates of black migration. Table 5 thus confirms and supplements Table 4 and uncovers the widespread net outmigrations that are partially concealed in low rates of white population increase in many central cities.

Table 6 is comparable to Table 4, except that it refers to suburban population changes. The diversity among metropolitan areas is obvious, and there is no need to supplement this table with another showing only the migration component of population growth.

TABLE 5

Net Migration to Central Cities,
Blacks Compared to Whites*
(1960 to 1970)

Net Migration Rate for Whites	Net Migration Rate for Blacks						
	Percent Loss			Percent Gain			
	−20% or Less	−10 to −20%	0 to −10%	0 to +10%	+10 to +20%	+20 to +30%	+30% or More
Percent loss:							
−20% or less		1	5	5	4	2	2
−10 to −20%			1	3	2	3	7
0 to −10%				2	5	3	1
Percent gain:							
0 to +10% ..			1	2		1	2
+10 to +20% ..			1	1	2	1	1
+20 to +30% ..	1						
+30% or more ..	1						

* Figures in the table are numbers of central cities. Net migration is expressed as a percentage of 1960 population. Rates for blacks refer to all nonwhites and not solely to blacks. The tally includes sixty of the 65 metropolitan areas having a total population in 1970 greater than five hundred thousand. For five areas with small black population, net migration estimates were not prepared. For four New England areas, the estimates refer to the central cities of the State Economic Area.

TABLE 6

Change in Suburban Population,
Blacks Compared to Whites*
(1960 to 1970)

| | | Change in Black Population | | |
| | | Percent Gain | | |
Change in White Population	Loss	0 to +25%	+25 to +50%	+50% or More
Loss	20	4	1	3
Percent gain:				
0 to +25%	27	21	10	29
+25 to +50%	8	17	5	38
+50% or more	2	15	7	9

* Figures in the table are numbers of metropolitan areas. The tally includes 216 metropolitan areas having a total population in 1970 greater than a hundred thousand. One area, Jacksonville, Florida, is excluded because the central city is co-extensive with Duval County and there is no suburban population.

At the beginning of this chapter, several reasons were advanced for focusing on rather elementary aspects of the changing black-white–city-suburb nexus. Among the reasons was the fact that results of the 1970 census are too recent for much new detailed analysis to have been completed. Many relevant studies have been published, drawing on the 1960 census data and other sources. By quoting selectively from a few of these earlier studies, one can widen and perhaps correct the focus.

Migration is a complex process, and it would be unfortunate if any remarks on black urbanization and white suburbanization served to reinforce the stereotype of poor blacks moving to the cities and rich whites fleeing to the suburbs. This particular stereotypical perspective is not only overly narrow, it is largely false. To quote from the abstracts of two studies that Alma Taeuber and I published in the mid-1960s; first, on black migration (1965, p. 429):

> ... During the 1955–60 period ... Negro in-migrants to a number of large cities, despite the presence of a socioeconomically depressed group of nonmetropolitan origin, were not of lower average socioeconomic status than the resident Negro population. Indeed, in educational attainment Negro in-migrants to northern cities were equal to or slightly higher than the resident white population. ... As the Negro population has changed from

a disadvantaged rural population to a metropolitan one of increasing socioeconomic levels, its patterns of migration have changed to become very much like those of the white population.

These white-black similarities in migration dynamics will also be found in studies of the 1960s and will become greater in the 1970s. Second, on white migration (1964, p. 718):

> Nearly all streams of migrants are of higher average socioeconomic status than nonmigrants. Large cities contribute to their suburbs and to other metropolitan areas more high-status migrants than they receive, whereas suburban rings receive more high-status migrants than they lose. This circulation of persons of higher levels of educational attainment and occupational status has the net effect of diminishing the socioeconomic level of central city populations and augmenting the socioeconomic level of suburban populations.

Other studies have shown that rates of outmigration from areas — both metropolitan and nonmetropolitan — tend to reflect primarily the age structure rather than the economic circumstances of the population. In our society the young leave home in search of different, if not better, opportunities. Areal differences in net migration arise primarily from where migrants settle rather than where they originate. New entrants to the labor force are in the ages of extraordinary geographic mobility. To a very large extent youth will seek jobs wherever they are, and conversely, jobs for the younger portion of the labor force may attract workers from a large area and not simply from a local labor market.

Just as a rather orderly national system of migration can produce effects that seem quite disorderly and disparate for differing racial and socioeconomic groups, so too can the process of metropolitan growth be viewed in a more orderly perspective than the jumble of city-suburb contrasts suggests. Suburbanization is simply urbanization occurring beyond the limits of the core municipality; and we might be better off if the special term had never come into common usage. Whether from the sociologists' traditional source, the Burgess zonal hypothesis, or from location economics, a model of metropolitan growth can be developed that calls for an evolutionary and never-ending process of relocation of social classes and types of residential areas. Schnore has elaborated on this theme in a number of papers, three of which are quoted, that apply this model to recent experience in the United States:

> Sheer age of settlement has emerged as the best predictor of the direction of city-suburb differences in socioeconomic

status. Older urbanized areas tend strongly to possess peripheral populations of higher socioeconomic standing than found in the central cities themselves. In contrast, newer cities tend to contain populations ranking higher on education, occupation, and income than their respective suburbs (Schnore, 1963, p. 82).

[If we look] at the nonwhite data . . . such relationships do tend to appear in the North and West. City-suburban status differentials . . . are generally similar to those shown by the white population in both broad regions. . . . The most probable reason why the southern nonwhites fail to show the usual city-suburban status differences is that in the South . . . the poorer and less advantaged nonwhite residents traditionally lived on the periphery of the city. . . . The southern nonwhite population . . . may be in a state of transition between the traditional residential pattern of the Old South and the contemporary American urban pattern seen in both white and nonwhite neighborhoods in the rest of the country (Palen and Schnore, 1965, p. 91).

. . . The nonwhite ghettos in large northern cities still tend to display the pattern observed earlier in . . . Chicago. That is, as distance increases from the center of the city, the socioeconomic status of nonwhite neighborhoods goes up. Nonwhite family income is higher, nonwhite educational levels mount, and the relative number of nonwhite males in "white-collar" employment increases (Schnore, 1965, p. 130).

A general model of population redistribution and evolving settlement patterns seems already to exist, and it does away with the centrality of distinctions between city and suburb and between black and white. The broad sweep of our demographic history may prove a simpler as well as a better guide to the dynamics of the changing labor force in the 1970s and beyond than we can get from short-term projections, using only the concepts provided by the current problem-oriented dialogue.

REFERENCES

Palen, J. John; and Schnore, Leo F. "Color Composition and City-Suburban Status Differences: A Replication and Extension." *Land Economics* (February 1965), vol. 41, no. 1.

Schnore, Leo F. "Social Class Segregation among Nonwhites in Metropolitan Areas." *Demography* (1965), vol. 2.

————. "The Socioeconomic Status of Cities and Suburbs." *American Sociological Review* (February 1963), vol. 28, no. 1.

Taeuber, Karl E.; and Taeuber, Alma F. "The Changing Character of Negro Migration." *American Journal of Sociology* (January 1965), vol. 70, no. 4.

——————. "White Migration and Socioeconomic Differences between Cities and Suburbs." *American Sociological Review* (October 1964), vol. 29, no. 5.

U.S. Department of Commerce, Bureau of the Census. *Census of Population, 1970.* Washington, D.C.: U.S. Government Printing Office. 1971.

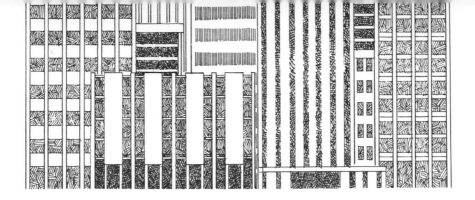

3
Suburban
Labor Markets

Thomas M. Stanback, Jr.*

It has become apparent that growth of population and employment in the suburbs of metropolitan areas has been a major source of social and economic change in the postwar American economy. This chapter examines these suburban economies — both the forces which have brought them about and the differences in their labor markets.

Significance of the Export Base, City Size, and Age

Urbanists have found it important to look upon cities as separate economies which export and import goods and services. This approach has given rise to what is often called the export base concept — the idea that cities are divided into two major sectors, an export sector and a local service sector. This concept is excessively simple but provides a valid starting point in the analysis of growth and development by underlining the basic fact that cities must export to survive. Moreover, when used with sophistication, it helps us understand how and why cities differ in terms of levels of income, spatial organization, and the special characteristics of their labor markets.

* Professor of economics, New York University, and senior research associate, Conservation of Human Resources, Columbia University. The findings set forth in this chapter are based upon research carried out in collaboration with Professor Richard V. Knight, Case Western Reserve University. The supporting evidence and a more detailed assessment of the findings will be presented in a forthcoming book.

In the export base concept, cities may be classified into three general types:

(1) Nodal centers — cities that exist principally to provide consumer and business services to outlying areas or hinterlands (i.e., centers for a combination of business services, transportation services, government, and frequently entertainment and cultural activities)

(2) Cities which primarily specialize in producing and exporting goods or some relatively restricted type of service (mostly manufacturing places)

(3) A number of cities whose exports are mixed

It is interesting to observe the extent to which the characteristics of cities are influenced by industrial structure. In the first place, income levels and the distribution of income are affected (Thompson, 1969). Manufacturing cities, at least those outside the South, tend to have somewhat higher than average median wages and to be characterized by a greater income equality. Moreover, their human resources differ and, with them, the composition of demand for goods and services. There are fewer professionals and fewer executives but also fewer low-level service workers, a smaller proportion of well-educated residents, and a lesser demand for cultural activities than in nodal places. Housing tends to reflect income both in terms of quality and size and of the degree of equality in housing standards.

W. R. Thompson, a leading urban economist and author of chapter 1, is fond of stating that "form follows function," meaning that the physical structure of the city is heavily influenced by its export base. Manufacturing-type places, since they provide comparatively few services, have relatively small central business districts. Moreover, they are likely to have fewer museums, theaters, and good restaurants. Their spatial organization will be less dense because there has never been the same fierce competition for access to the center of the city where transportation and face-to-face communication have traditionally been maximized. Finally, public transportation is typically less well developed, since there is not the same need to connect all areas with the center city. For nodal places the central business district will be larger, denser, more diversified, more dominant, and better integrated with the remainder of the metropolitan area through public transportation.

All of this must be qualified for us to recognize the influence of size. Large cities are more diversified for a number of reasons, including the fact that the sheer size of markets encourages a variety of producers of goods and services. Large places, even large nodal places, will typically have a sizable manufacturing sector. In addition, as the city grows the flow of traffic and the transportation system must be disproportionately enlarged. Public transportation both within the city and to outlying areas is likely to play a more important role.

Finally, a city's age influences its spatial organization. Older places were oriented to rail, water, and streetcar transportation when spatial organization was determined. Younger cities have developed largely in the age of automobile transportation. The former are characterized by greater density and tight grid-like layout of streets; the latter by less density and greater orientation to clusters of specialized activity, frequently at major intersections of highways.

The Suburban Economy

The above sketch provides insights which are important in analyzing suburban growth and industrial composition. Though a part of the overall metropolitan economy, the suburb may also be examined as if it were a separate economy. It exports to the city and to the outside world. Moreover, it has a local sector as well as an export sector. Growth takes place through enlargement of these sectors and may be accelerated by import substitution. It is encouraged by the increase in external economies and by the development of its economic, its political, and its social infrastructure.

The suburban economy will be influenced by its adjacent city. Its export firms may have migrated from the city or been attracted to the area by the city's and the region's markets, labor force, transportation facilities, and raw materials. Its local sector is influenced by the level of income and other characteristics of that portion of the city's work force which it houses.

Industrial Composition

Among the ten SMSAs studied (Atlanta, Baltimore, Boston, Cleveland, Denver, Houston, New Orleans, New York, Philadelphia, and St. Louis), industrial composition of employment in cities and their respective suburbs showed significant similarities as well as fundamental differences (U.S. Department of Health, Education and Welfare, Social Security Administration, various years; U.S. Bureau of the Census, various years; and U.S. Bureau of Labor Statistics, various years). Suburbs tend to take on the industrial coloration of the cities they surround. Where manufacturing employment is relatively large in the city (as in Cleveland), it tends to be relatively large in the suburbs; and where city employment is specialized in business services, the corresponding percentage of suburban employment in these activities also tends to be relatively high. On the other hand, nothing is clearer than that cities and suburbs differ in industrial composition, especially in manufacturing and consumer services which comprise a significantly larger share of suburban employment.

This fact is explained by two of the major processes which have accounted for the revolutionary growth of the suburbs: the growth of manufacturing through movement of manufacturers from the city (and subsequent independent growth) and the shift in residential location from city to suburb of middle- and upper-income families whose principal source of employment is within the city's economy. Accordingly, the major export base of suburbs has tended to be manufacturing and the income generated by commuters (a "hidden" export). The former has given rise to a relatively large manufacturing sector, the latter to a relatively large consumer services sector serving both those who live and work in the suburbs and those who live in the suburbs and work in the city.

In addition, construction employment has tended to be relatively larger in suburbs, reflecting the very rapid growth and need for construction of all kinds. On the other hand, business service employment is relatively smaller in suburbs, reflecting the continued locational preference of central business districts for these activities, despite certain tendencies for them to relocate in the suburbs.

The Nature of Suburban Development

Two additional observations are necessary for understanding the nature of suburban development. First, both the spatial organization and special characteristics of the suburban economy have been in large measure the result of the revolutionary increase in the use of automotive transportation in the postwar period and of certain new institutions which have come into being as a result of this change. Second, suburbanization has involved processes of economic and social selection and adaptation which have resulted in fundamental differences in functions performed in cities and suburbs and in the types of employment opportunities which each affords.

Impact of Increased Automotive Transportation

It is difficult to overestimate the role played by increased car and truck ownership, coupled with the development of the highway system. On the one hand, the rise of automotive transportation has released both individuals and firms from the need for close proximity to the city; on the other, it has brought about a new set of locational requirements and a different sort of spatial organization.

Manufacturing plants seek to maximize access to major highways; retail shopping centers are built at or near high traffic intersections; and office activities tend to be organized round campus locations or office complexes with access to throughways and other major arteries. At the same time, the location of housing is influenced by the ability of developers to put together sizable tracts of land which tie into the highway matrix and permit construction at acceptable prices.

The major shopping center was developed to maximize market coverage by centrality in terms of highway access. Through such maximization it attains sales volumes which permit firms to draw off trade from central business districts of both the central city and suburban cities and towns. The industrial park and to a lesser degree the office park provide a convenient package of modern facilities, suburban land, transportation access, and needed utilities. Location in suburbia becomes convenient for even the small firm. The result of these developments is a labor market for which the automobile is the major mode of transportation; for employees of many firms it is the only mode.

Selective and Adaptive Process in Suburbanization

Growth and development of the suburban economy have been accomplished through a series of selective and adaptive economic, social, and political decisions which have resulted in an economy which differs sharply in its essential characteristics from that of the central city and which gives rise to a significantly different labor market. This may be seen readily in the case of manufacturing growth.

Manufacturers located in the suburbs tend to represent the growing edge of the economy. In general, they are the technologically most progressive and the best heeled. Analysis of average wages of production workers in the ten SMSAs studied showed that suburban workers were paid higher hourly wages in suburbs than cities and worked more hours each year.

In the retail trades, growth in the suburbs has adapted itself to the market. Suburban retailing takes place partly in a large number of stores in neighborhoods and small business districts, where traffic is low, and partly in shopping centers, where substantial volumes of trade are generated. Comparison of size of firm and average annual income of employees indicates no tendency for firms to be either larger or smaller in suburbs than in cities, but does indicate that annual earnings per worker are smaller. It is likely that these differentials in earnings stem from more than a single cause. Clearly, much of suburban retailing is relatively inefficient in terms of sales volume per employee, and this would tend to lower the wage in retailing. A more important cause, however, may be the marked tendency to employ large numbers of relatively young people and middle-aged women and to employ them on less than a full-time basis.

Data relating to other consumer and business services also indicate that annual earnings are lower in suburbs. Explanations once again arise from the basic economics of product and labor markets. Size of firm data show service firms to be smaller in suburbs than in cities. The reason lies in the scattered nature of markets. Since services must be rendered directly to user, a lack of concentration of markets necessitates the small firm and with it, in many instances, a tendency toward lower productivity. In addition, here, as in retailing, there is a heavy reliance on young workers and middle-aged women and a tendency to employ them on a part-time basis.

It is in office and headquarters activity that we witness some of the most interesting cases of special adaptation. While there has been a lively movement of these activities to the suburb, such a movement represents a selected group of firms whose operations and needs are of such a nature as to permit ready adjustment to the suburban economy. Also, there is considerable evidence that office activities which are "spun off" to the suburbs represent relatively routine operations requiring large proportions of low clerical skills and foreman-type supervision but small proportions of executive talent.

On the other hand, headquarters and research and development operations which have located in the suburbs represent a relatively rich mix of executive and professional talent, compared to routine clerical and supervisory skills. Interviews indicate, however, that until now there has been a selective process at work in the location of these activities. Essentially, the headquarters and research operations which locate in the suburbs are those which find themselves relatively free of a need to take advantage of the external economies and face-to-face communications which can be maximized in the central business district. Frequently, they are oriented mainly to their operating divisions in other parts of the region or nation and can perform their business district-related functions by maintaining limited facilities within the city.

Finally, there has been a process of social, political, and economic constraint at work which has acted to prevent any substantial movement of blacks to the suburbs. Through zoning, bias, and simply the high cost of building homes and commuting, racial minorities have been limited to a relatively small role in suburbia.

In the face of these constraints some adaptation has been made by the minorities concerned. The principal adaptation has been through commutation, discussed below. In the main, suburbs continue to be characterized by limited racial minorities that find themselves largely confined to small suburban ghettos.

CHARACTERISTICS OF THE SUBURBAN LABOR MARKET

What we have seen of the special nature of the suburbs suggests several generalizations about the nature of demand and supply forces at work in suburban labor markets. Demand stems from two principal sources. The first is demand from the manufacturing sector (accounting for from 22 to 48 percent of employment in the ten suburbs studied). Suburban plants are likely to be relatively modern and more productive than city plants. Moreover, as noted above, they are frequently located at considerable distance from the home of the worker.

The second principal source of demand is the consumer service sector (accounting for 29 to 43 percent of employment). This relatively heavy demand arises from the highly residentiary character of the suburbs. In contrast to the manufacturing sector, these jobs are likely to be poorly paid, justifying only relatively short journeys to work.

Thus the two major sources of demand for labor stand in sharp contrast — the one offering relatively high, the other relatively low wages. Of course there are other sources of demand, but they play a lesser role. Business services, through a rapidly growing sector, are still small in comparison to those in cities. Construction is somewhat larger for suburbs than for cities because of the higher growth rates in the former. Nevertheless, in most suburbs it accounted for less than a tenth of covered employment in 1970.

When we turn to the supply side, we note that the mass movement of middle-class Americans to the suburbs has influenced the suburban labor market in at least two significant ways. In the first place, it has created an economy in which an important segment of the labor force — the daily commuter — is employed elsewhere. Under such conditions the suburban employer must either look to the remainder of the eligible labor force for his or her workers, draw upon commuters from the city or from exurbia, or compete with city employers for commuters from the suburbs. Accordingly, we might expect a different final mix within the work force in terms of sex and age from that which exists in the city.

A second way is by affecting the supply of female labor. If the suburban society is characterized by a disproportionately large share of women from the middle class who are engaged in responsibilities of the home during the years of child bearing and raising and who are available for part- or full-time work only in their early adult and middle years, then to that extent, the supply of labor will differ between city and suburb. These general observations regarding demand and supply characteristics prompt the discussion below.

Age Composition of Employment

We must recognize at the outset that suburban populations tend to be somewhat younger than city populations. But even after these differences have been adjusted, distributions among age classes differ sharply among comparable sex-age groups. For white males, shares of employment are relatively larger in suburbs than in the city for those below 25 years of age, smaller for those 25 to 44 years of age, and approximately the same for those 45 to 64 years of age.

These findings reflect, it is presumed, the effect of commutation. To the extent that sizable numbers of mature, white suburban males find employment in the city and younger workers do not, the percentage of suburban workers in the older age groups will be reduced and the percentage in the younger age brackets will be increased. At the same time, but to a lesser degree, the percentage of young white males in the cities will be decreased and the percentage of older workers increased.

Among black males under 25 years, the share of employment is significantly smaller in the suburbs than in the city and slightly larger in each of the other age brackets. Two explanations can be offered for this observation, neither of necessity excluding the other. First, the substantial flows of black commuters from city to suburb serve to swell disproportionately the ranks of employed blacks over 25 years of age, thereby reducing the percentage of workers under 25 in the suburb and (to a much lesser extent) increasing the percentage of black workers under 25 in the city. This is of course the opposite of the explanation offered above for city-suburban differences in percentages of white males in the under 25 years bracket. Second, young black males fare less well in suburbs than in cities, possibly because low-level jobs in the consumer services are difficult to reach from suburban ghettos or because they compete with young whites in a setting which is overwhelmingly white.

For suburban white females, we observe a strong tendency for young women to leave the work force during the years when children are being raised and to return in considerable numbers in the years that follow. As for black females, shares of employment in the several age brackets do not differ significantly from city to suburb. Patterns of employment by age in both city and suburb are well established: lowest share of employment in the under twenty bracket, highest share in the twenty to 25 bracket, with shares progressively lower in each of the higher age brackets. In neither city nor suburb do black women have the tendency shown by white women to leave the work force and return in middle life.

Female Employment

One way in which differences between city and suburban economies may be highlighted is by comparing the importance of female employment. Women tend to be employed in greater numbers in those activities where secretarial and clerical skills are needed, in nonprofessional service activities, and in branches of manufacturing where work is repetitive and value added is relatively low (typically in nondurables).

Cities employ a higher percentage of females than do suburbs. In general, the principal structural characteristics which contribute to this basic difference between city and suburb are the relatively high proportion of total employment in manufacturing and construction in suburbs and the relatively high proportion of business services in the cities. Manufacturing and construction employ on the average a relatively small percentage of women; business services, a relatively large percentage. The resulting tendency for cities to employ relatively more women is only partially offset by the fact that the consumer services category, which is more important in the suburb, employs a relatively large number of women.

The above summary statement of effect of industrial composition in terms of major groupings provides, however, only a rough description. We must recognize also the effects of employment distribution among subcategories *within* industrial groupings. One of the most interesting observations to be made is that female employment percentages in manufacturing are smaller for suburbs. The explanation clearly must be that the types of manufacturing which flourish in the suburbs are those in which women are not employed in large numbers — presumably industries with relatively large inputs of capital, high skill levels, and high wages. We must conclude that the structure of the manufacturing sector in suburbs, at least among most of the metropolitan areas studied, does not favor employment of females, although the larger relative size of the manufacturing sector acts *ceteris paribus* to enlarge such employment.

Within the consumer services group, female employment percentages also tend to be greater in cities. This means of course that cities tend to have relatively large shares of consumer service employment in activities for which female employment percentages are large — activities such as personal services, nonprofit membership organizations, and retailing which specializes in general merchandise, apparel, and accessories.

Industrial Composition of Employment by Sex and Race

Perhaps the most direct way to compare city and suburban labor markets is to examine the industrial composition of the major sex-race segments of the work force (i.e., white males, black males, white females, black females).

In virtually every comparison white males in suburbs have higher percentages of their employment in manufacturing and in consumer services than is the case in cities. Black males, on the other hand, tend to have higher percentages of employment in manufacturing in suburbs but lower percentages of employment in consumer services. Thus black males appear to have relatively good access to manufacturing jobs in the suburbs (though not necessarily to the best manufacturing jobs) but relatively poor access to consumer service jobs. The earlier evidence regarding age structure of employment suggests that this lack of access takes the form of restricted entry of young suburban blacks into the jobs for which inexperienced young people are most eligible, jobs in retailing and other consumer services.

Comparisons between white women and black women tell us something of the essential characteristics of the industrial composition of the female work force. White women find relatively more jobs than black women in business services in both city and suburb; black women, relatively more jobs in consumer services. In manufacturing, however, experience varies widely from place to place, and there is no clear-cut tendency for women of either race to have a relatively larger share of total employment in this category.

It is interesting that black women in the suburbs do not face the same obstacles, compared to white women, in consumer services employment that black men compared to white men face. Apparently, there is not the same restriction of access. In párt this is no doubt due to the fact that black women are more frequently hired as domestics, a relatively important occupation in the affluent suburbs. It may be due also in part to the nature of the jobs they typically fill. As both women and blacks they are the lowest paid group in the total work force, performing menial services in hospitals, retail stores, motels, and restaurants. If there are constraints due to difficulty of competing for jobs in the dispersed suburban economy, there are very likely offsetting factors arising from the large demand for low-wage menials in a heavily consumer service-oriented economy.

Commuting Patterns, Labor Force Participation, and Unemployment

To the extent that workers in the suburbs find employment in and commute to the city, suburban employers are affected. The supply of labor is reduced and the labor market, all other things equal, is tightened. City employers are similarly affected by city dwellers commuting to jobs outside the metropolis.

When we examine the race, sex, and age characteristics of these commuter flows, we observe that:

(1) The flow of black commuters is largely from city to suburb — the opposite of major flows for whites.

(2) Commuting flows both to cities and to suburbs are disproportionately small for workers under 25 years of age.

(3) The percentage of the female work force comprised of commuters in the city is smaller than the comparable percentage for the male work force (and smaller than women's share of the work force).

These findings are not unexpected, for they arise largely as a result of two well-known facts: Workers will travel farther to well-paying jobs than to poorly paying ones (distant jobs that are difficult to search out and are expensive and time consuming to reach must be rewarded by higher pay); and blacks have restricted opportunities to reside in the suburbs. It follows that male job opportunities, which typically offer significantly higher pay, will attract more commuters than female job opportunities and jobs for which young people (male and female) are eligible, since the latter typically offer low pay and frequently only part-time employment.

Among white males, participation rates are systematically higher and unemployment rates lower in suburbs than in cities. This reflects in part the social processes at work in the suburb — its rapid settlement in recent times by middle-class families with stable employment and its tendencies to exclude minority groups and other poor. There can be little doubt that it reflects also the effect of suburb-to-city commuting on the availability to the suburban employer of that type of worker who makes up most of the daily commuting public, the white male employee. When this segment of the labor force is drawn off to the city, supply shortages develop which are reflected in higher labor force participation rates and lower unemployment rates.

Among black males, participation rates are not consistently higher in the suburbs. Yet black male unemployment rates are lower in suburbs than in cities in almost every comparison. This suggests that although a substantial portion of the potential black labor force does not participate, employment opportunities are better in suburbs than in cities for that portion which does participate.

Participation rates for black males, however, are sharply lower than for white males in all suburban labor markets. Clearly, the average black suburban male worker stands in a position more sharply differentiated from his white counterpart than does the black male worker in the city. On the one hand, the white male worker of the suburb is likely to be actively engaged in the labor market. Facing opportunities for employment in both city and suburb, he represents a class of worker for whom labor participation rates are high. On the other, the typical black suburban worker, eligible typically for only low-level jobs in the city (which do not justify expensive commuting), looks for employment within the suburban economy. (There is of course a small but growing black middle class in the suburbs.) If his situation is slightly better than for his black counterpart in the city, it is nonetheless sharply inferior to that of his white counterpart in the suburbs.

When data for female workers are examined, we find that white women have lower participation rates in suburbs than cities, reflecting, it is presumed, the significantly large number of women who perform roles as housewives outside the labor force. Unemployment rates are roughly the same in city and suburb, indicating a general tendency for jobs to be more or less equally available to white women seeking employment in one area as in the other.

Significantly, city-suburb differences in participation rates and unemployment rates of black women are not apparent. However, both participation rates and unemployment rates are higher for blacks in almost every comparison between black women and white women in cities and in suburbs. Black women everywhere find it necessary to enter the labor market in relatively larger numbers than do white women and experience greater difficulties in finding and holding employment once they have entered.

Stability of Employment

Using a somewhat limited measure derived from Social Security data, we found that the suburban economy is characterized by less stable employment than the city economy. This finding does not hold, however, with equal strength for each sex-race category. It is less marked, for example, for white males than for white females, who tend to find more stable employment in the city at every age.

When we examined industry groups, we found that for white males, and to a lesser extent white females, stability of employment in manufacturing is higher in most suburbs than in adjacent cities. In the business services, however, the evidence pointed to a tendency toward greater employment stability in city than in suburbs. In the consumer services, there is a clear predominance of stable jobs in the cities. For blacks, sample size is less adequate. Findings are tentative and available only for males. It appears that employment of males is more stable in cities.

All of this goes far to confirm the picture that has progressively emerged from the preceding analyses. Suburban economies tend to be characterized by a dichotomy of good jobs and poor jobs. On the one hand, there are the relatively well-paid jobs in manufacturing, where wages are high and work stable, along with a select group of professional and executive jobs. On the other hand, there is a large group of consumer service jobs which are characterized by relatively low pay and a high incidence of unstable employment. As noted above, these jobs are filled largely by young white workers of both sexes and by middle-aged women. The special problem of blacks apparently is that although employment is open to them in the manufacturing sector, it tends to be available only to those in the prime working ages. To the extent that jobs in the service trades can be reached and are available, they provide an entry point into the work force for young blacks as well as young whites. But business service jobs are in fact rarely available to blacks, and consumer service jobs are filled to a disproportionate extent by young whites.

Significance of Suburban Cities and Towns

One of the principal arguments thus far has been that spatially the suburban economy is organized in such a way as to discriminate frequently against the young and old — and the poor, generally — by reducing access to jobs. The discussion has proceeded, however, without explicit recognition that the suburban economy is organized to a marked extent around towns and cities. These places provide schools, medical services, police, fire protection, and utilities, as well as a variety of business and consumer services. In addition, some suburban places are actually satellite cities of considerable size which have served (in years before rapid suburbanization) as important service or industrial centers.

Towns and cities of course represent a greater clustering of residential and economic functions than is found elsewhere. There is a greater tendency in larger places for rich and poor to live in relative proximity to one another and to share residentiary services in both the public and private sectors. Such spatial and economic organization, in turn, tends to favor the poor by increasing the choice of employment and by reducing the length of the journey to work. To what extent, then, does the existence of towns and small cities within suburban areas tend to reduce the problems of sprawl and to ameliorate labor market conditions?

From evidence that was available for the metropolitan areas under study, it would appear that such urban agglomerations within suburbs do not significantly alter previous generalizations. A first reason is that these places play a secondary role in terms of total population housed and served. Among the ten suburban rings only three (Boston, Denver, and New Orleans) show more than 23 percent of total population residing in cities of fifty thousand or more, and only one (Denver) shows more than 45 percent of total population residing in cities of 25,000 or more. In short, a majority of suburbanites resides in small towns or outside town or city limits.

Second, suburban towns and cities tend to be socially homogeneous, varying widely in terms of the typical income of residents. Some places such as Shaker Heights (Cleveland) and Bronxville (New York) are predominantly high-income suburbs, while others such as East Cleveland, Lynn (Boston), and Essex (Baltimore) are low income. Thus, among the poor, spatial organization tends to limit job opportunities to those areas in which they reside and in which consumer and public sector expenditures offer the least promise for rewarding employment.

Third, suburban towns and cities are themselves very loosely organized spatially and are served by inadequate public transportation. The most recent census data indicate that the percentage of workers using private cars in the journey to work differs little between most cities or towns and the remainder of the counties in which they are located.

Finally, cities and towns serve as the focal points of only a fraction of suburban economic activity. To be sure, local public services as well as downtown and neighborhood shopping are located within these places. In some instances, as in White Plains, New York, the heart of the city is a major shopping center. On the other hand, the large retail center, located away from the center of town and poorly served by public transportation, has gone far to reduce the role of the suburban city's downtown shopping area. Data from the *Census of Business* show that in 1967 major retail centers (with rare exceptions, shopping centers located away from downtown areas) accounted for 24 to 36 percent of total retail sales in eight of the ten suburban areas studied. Also, offices as well as manufacturing plants have tended to locate outside towns and cities and near major highways. Even hospitals and colleges have demonstrated such tendencies. In short, suburban areas are indeed heterogeneous and more complex than previous simplified assumptions would indicate. Nevertheless, there appears to be little reason to question on these grounds the observations made thus far.

SUBURBAN LABOR MARKETS UNDER CONDITIONS OF GROWTH AND CHANGE

In the first section, attention was directed to the processes of urban growth and the importance of the export sector in determining the distinctive characteristics of industrial and occupational distribution of employment and of spatial organization of the city's economy. Following this, we discussed the special nature of the suburban economy, noting its tendency to take on much of the industrial coloration of the central city while at the same time showing larger shares of employment in manufacturing, construction, and consumer services and smaller shares in business services and professional activities. We noted further the heavy dependence on trucks and private cars, the tendency toward sprawl, and the selective and adaptive growth processes which have resulted in a suburban economy in which there are a relatively few high-level professional jobs, a disproportionate number of fairly well-paying jobs in manufacturing plants which are largely modern and efficient, and a large number of low-paying service jobs (principally consumer services).

In the preceding section we discussed special characteristics of the suburban work force in terms of labor force participation, age, sex, and race distribution of employment, and the industrial composition of employment in each sex-race category. Principal findings were that suburban economies, largely because of industrial composition, employ fewer women than corresponding city economies, that the suburban work force is comprised to a larger extent of young people under 25 and of middle-aged women, and that there are important differences in the role of blacks and whites within the work force. Regarding this last item, it was observed that although black males of prime working age are able to find manufacturing jobs in proportion to their share of the population, those under 25 are underemployed in the large consumer services sector where the majority of entry-level jobs exists. Moreover, blacks of all ages are underrepresented in business services in the suburbs, as is also true for blacks in the city.

If these observations highlight the nature of the suburban economy and its work force, what can be said of the way in which the suburban work force has adapted to growth and change? What problems lie ahead for the suburban economy?

During the decade of the 1960s, the suburban economies studied grew rapidly, especially in the period 1965 to 1970, when net growth in employment ranged from 20 to 98 percent. Although it is beyond the scope of this chapter to analyze the processes by which such growth occurred, it is important to note the evidence at hand regarding the responsiveness of the work force to growth. Growth has been fed from three streams: new entrants (those who were not on the Social Security rolls at the beginning of the five-year period), entrants from the city (those working in the city at the beginning of the period but in the suburban work force at the end), and entrants from elsewhere (those working outside the SMSA at the beginning of the period but in the suburban work force at the end). The first of these groups is composed largely of young people under 25, with a substantial number of white women over 35 years of age.

Among these three groups, the largest on the average is new entrants, with entrants from elsewhere second and entrants from the city third. (All rates of entry as well as rates of net change are computed by dividing the number of entrants during the five-year period by total employment at the beginning of the period.) The astonishing finding is the extreme elasticity of the rate of new entry, which varies in rough conformity with the rate of net change in employment. In the more slowly growing suburban economies, such as Boston and Cleveland, it ranged between 42 and 47 percent. In the two fastest growing suburban areas, Atlanta and Denver, it attained levels of 78 and 81 percent, respectively. Even when growth was extremely rapid, new entrants flowed into the work force. What the data tell us is that recent growth has been made possible to a large extent by drawing upon new entrants, with substantial additions by in-migration, especially in the fast-growing places.

From this evidence and from what has been shown regarding the industrial composition and age, sex, and race characteristics of the suburban economy, it would appear that employers have not experienced great difficulty in finding workers. Relatively well-paying manufacturing jobs have been readily filled by workers, white and black, from suburb, city, and elsewhere. (When manufacturers move to the suburbs from the city, production workers tend to follow.) Poorly paying consumer and business service jobs have been manned largely by young whites and white women in middle life. To the extent that office and headquarters activities have located in the suburbs, more women have been able to compete for secretarial and clerical labor in a market where there was a relatively smaller demand for women than in a city.

In qualitative terms, the populace that makes up the suburban labor market, being disproportionately middle to upper income, is generally better educated than that of the city and, in all likelihood, more readily adaptable to the routines of the workplace. It is probable that such a pool of workers is lacking in certain specific skills (e.g., there have been some complaints of an inadequate supply of experienced secretaries), but such deficiencies may usually be overcome by their being trained or acquiring experience within the firm.

Yet it is not clear that the suburban job market has been well suited to the needs of all segments of the potential labor force. When we visualize the suburban economy with its large numbers of small retail and service firms scattered along highway strip developments, in neighborhood shopping centers, and in major shopping centers and office and industrial parks, it is clear that the poor — especially minorities and the elderly who do not have cars or access to car pools — have difficulty locating jobs and commuting to work. Faced with inadequate public transportation, a large segment of the work force finds that the journey to work is time consuming and expensive. This raises a serious issue regarding growth and development of the suburbs in the years ahead.

If suburban economies are inefficiently organized spatially, giving rise to patterns of the journey to work involving a maze of crisscross trips, heavy burdens on highway arteries, and little opportunity for development of a workable system of public transportation, it is difficult to see how these economies can avoid serious problems of matching jobs and people under conditions of continued high growth rates. It is even more difficult to imagine that a situation can continue indefinitely in which the poor must live in the central city, while the jobs which they are best equipped to fill are opening up in the suburbs. Already we witness court battles to prevent firms from setting up shop in the suburbs with no provision for the housing of their workers. The battle for housing that is more open may be expected to be increasingly a concomitant of suburban growth.

Finally, if an already difficult and inequitable transportation situation is complicated by the need to curtail sharply the use of private automobiles in order to conserve energy and to meet environmental standards, the suburbs probably face serious problems. New patterns of spatial organization will be required which will emphasize concentrations of economic and residential activity to bring workers and jobs closer together and to facilitate the use of public transportation. Under such conditions it is not unlikely that the central city will experience some improvement in its competitive position.

The period ahead holds opportunities for more orderly development of city and suburb as an integrated metropolitan area than we have known thus far. What is called for is a recognition of the symbiosis that exists between the two.

In terms of economic function, the city and suburbs are interdependent. In terms of amenities, the two can be complementary and can provide opportunities for alternative life-styles for their residents. To work toward a more logical and humane organization of metropolitan economies is a major challenge for the remaining years of this century.

References

Thompson, Wilbur R. "The Economic Base of Urban Problems." In *Contemporary Economic Issues.* Edited by N. W. Chamberlain. Homewood, Illinois: Richard Irwin, Inc. 1969.

U.S. Department of Commerce, Bureau of the Census. *Census of the Population.* Washington, D.C.: U.S. Government Printing Office. Various years.

U.S. Department of Health, Education and Welfare, Social Security Administration. *Continuous Work History Sample.* Washington, D.C.: U.S. Government Printing Office. Various years.

U.S. Department of Labor, Bureau of Labor Statistics. *Census of Business.* Washington, D.C.: U.S. Government Printing Office. Various years.

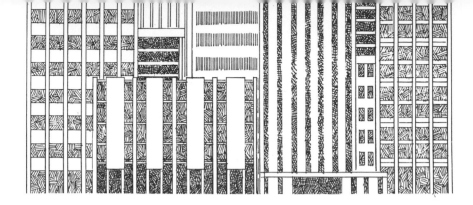

4
The Public Economy of the Metropolis

DICK NETZER*

During the 1960s, the public economy of the metropolis labored under well-advertised stresses, difficulties that were most evident in the large central cities of the North and West: It was hell to be mayor, and not much better to be governor. Public expenditure in metropolitan areas increased rapidly, partly in response to an underlying increase in the public work to be done (holding the scope and quality of public services constant), but more in response to changing social perceptions of what *should* be done and to increases in the unit costs of public services, notably increased public sector salary levels. For the large central cities, the fiscal pressures associated with the expenditure increase were compounded by the apparent acceleration in the rate of decentralization of economic activity within urban areas, thus diminishing the relative taxable capacity of most large cities. However, the accounts were balanced more or less by increased rates of local taxation and even more by a large increase in the flow of public funds from external sources: state and federal governments.

These fiscal developments in the public economy had significant employment and manpower effects, the most striking of which were positive: There was rapid expansion in public sector employment, providing substantial new job opportunities for minority groups, among others. In the central cities, this often did no more than offset the net loss in

* Dean, Graduate School of Public Administration, New York University.

71

manufacturing and other private sector employment in aggregate terms, but on the whole the new public sector jobs were better than the private sector jobs lost to the central cities, for the rise in average salary levels in the public sector was significantly larger than that in the private sector. It appears that today local government compensation levels in a wide array of job categories in large cities are well above the appropriate private sector counterparts.

The data are clear. Between 1961 and 1971, local government employment increased by two million, nearly 50 percent, with somewhat more than half the increase occurring in the 72 largest metropolitan areas and sizable increases in central cities, despite stable or declining populations. State government employment, much of it located in the larger metropolitan areas, increased even more rapidly. Meanwhile, private sector employment increased by only 23 percent; the private sector increase was less than this in the largest metropolitan areas and negligible or negative in most large central cities. Average annual earnings for local government employees increased by 74 percent, compared to a 62 percent private sector increase. In 1961, average earnings in public and private sector employment were virtually equal; by 1971, earnings in local government employment averaged about 10 percent above the private sector level.

But there were negative effects not independent of the positive ones. The increases in local government payrolls contributed to the fiscal stress, notably in the form of increased central city taxes and continual threats of even more increases, and this in turn affected private location decisions. Hard evidence on this is not easy to find, but there is some. For example, a careful econometric study of the effects of the New York City sales tax produced evidence which suggests that the increase of one percentage point in the tax rate in 1963 cost the city's economy nearly ten thousand jobs in retail trade by diverting sales to suburban locations (Levin, 1966, pp. 635–91; the employment estimate is mine). In the suburbs, fiscal pressures heavily conditioned decisions on land-use controls, with effects on private location decisions and thus on employment.

The Metropolitan Fisc

It is appropriate to examine the essential nature of the metropolitan fiscal problem in the United States as it is customarily defined by scholars. To begin with, the American system of government assigns a considerable share of total public sector responsibilities to local governments, and this is especially marked for the larger central cities. Costly functions that are directly performed by central or provincial governments in most other advanced countries are assigned to local units here, and large central cities tend to be responsible for activities handled by state agencies outside the central cities, or not done at all by any public agency beyond the central cities. There is of course a fair amount of external fiscal support of these activities — and this support greatly increased during the 1960s and early 1970s — but the local level is left with a substantial job of financing public services from locally raised funds. Thus in 1970 to 1971, local governments accounted for 41 percent of total civilian public expenditure and financed, from their own resources, 28 percent of all civilian public expenditure.

Because American metropolitan areas are rich, the local finance problem is not inherently overwhelming. The difficulty is that we do not have local government machinery that can tap the entire income and wealth of metropolitan areas. Instead, our metropolitan areas are divided into a large number of separate political and taxing units that contain unequal amounts of taxable income and wealth and that confront unequal requirements for local government services. The average metropolitan area with a population of five hundred thousand or more had 184 separate local government units in 1972.

But even this degree of fragmentation of the metropolitan fisc would not cause anything like the difficulties it does if the local government fiscal responsibilities did not involve so much income redistribution in money or in kind. The fact is that roughly one-third of the expenditures of the municipal governments in the cities with populations of three hundred thousand or more involves functions that are heavily affected with income redistribution goals; almost half of this expenditure is financed from fiscal resources of local, rather than state and federal, governments. One result is that we are asking some truly poor central cities — the Newarks — to tax the poor in order to redistribute income to the poor. More generally, the more affluent residents of central cities as well as many types of businesses can and do vote with their feet against being taxed to redistribute income, by the simple expedient of moving to parts of the metropolitan area where the population characteristics are such that much less income redistribution is called for. Here, too, the hard evidence is limited, but some empirical verification of a proposition that is logically unassailable does exist (Aronson and Schwartz, 1973, pp. 137–60).

The relatively recent phenomenon of collective bargaining with public employees appreciably aggravates the situation. This development naturally came first and has proceeded farthest in the larger central cities. It has produced the high rate of increase in local government compensation levels noted earlier, and there is no reason to think this source of fiscal pressure will abate, given the considerable combined economic and political bargaining power on the employee side and the evident weakness on the employer side. It should be noted that some of the salary pressures of recent years have an economic basis that would exist even in the absence of collective bargaining, for relatively large increases in compensation are always essential in one sector if that sector is to bid labor away from other sectors (which has been happening in the public sector for a quarter of a century). There are signs that the intersector transfer of labor will be much less a source of pressure in the decade ahead, but the monopoly power of public employee unions remains.

Fiscal reformers have offered no solutions to this last problem, but there is a set of conventional solutions to the other structural problems of the metropolitan fisc to be found in the large volume of literature on the subject (Netzer, 1968, pp. 435–76). The conventional wisdom begins with the proposition that *all* public expenditures made primarily for income redistribution reasons — including income maintenance programs, health services to the poor, housing and related subsidies, and the major element in school finance that is redistributive in purpose, among other things — should be financed by the federal government, as is done in most other advanced economies. Second, the provision or the financing of public services whose benefits and costs necessarily, because of technological characteristics, spill over local government boundaries should be on a regional basis. This does not always require the fashioning of new governmental entities that operate at the regional scale, for we do possess existing governmental entities empowered to substitute for regional government for most purposes — the state governments themselves, that can intervene (and increasingly are intervening) in such regional concerns as transportation and environmental protection.

The required upward shifting of governmental responsibilities can be accomplished in different ways. One is the outright transfer of responsibility for provision of the service: federalization of the welfare system, national health insurance, and state government transportation authorities (the actual case in New York and Massachusetts). Another is the expansion of grants to the local government service providers, with the external grant set at levels which reflect the proportion of the benefits from provision of the service that is external to the local government jurisdiction. Note that this calls for grants that are quite specific in purpose, not block grants for a broad category of activities like "transportation" or "community development," categories that comprehend a good many specific activities whose costs and benefits are entirely internal to a given local jurisdiction. The truly valid criticism of the vast array of highly specific grants that evolved before the advent of the Nixon Administration is not that they were too specific but that many of them were for programs in which there was no real nationwide interest — and some were just plain ineffective, whatever the balance of presumed internal and external benefits.

Another concern of conventional fiscal reformers has been inequality of fiscal resources and its consequences, inequality among states, between central cities and suburbs, and among local units generally. The usual prescription is for *equalizing* grants from higher levels of government, in addition to fiscal transfers designed to *optimize* the output of public services, which is the type of arrangement discussed in the preceding paragraph. General revenue sharing in concept is a form of equalizing grant, with a formula that is meant to reflect both differences in fiscal capacity and differences in needs for public revenue. The formula actually employed for federal revenue sharing is far from perfect in these regards, but it should be noted that the complexity and diversity in the American system of government are such that it is virtually impossible to devise any formula that is entirely satisfactory on a nationwide basis.

The most important type of state aid to local government — state aid for schools — also is heavily affected with equalization purposes; indeed, equalization is the historic goal of state school aid, although many states do a poor job of it. Equalization can also be promoted by shifts in functional responsibility, such as statewide school financing — as has been proposed in a number of states (New York, New Jersey, and Michigan) and very nearly exists in Minnesota — or assignment of responsibilities to area-wide agencies able to tax over whole metropolitan areas or regions.

One aspect of the fiscal disparity problem deserves special mention, for it concerns the most important local government fiscal resource: the property tax. If the governance of the metropolis is highly fragmented among a large number of political units, many of them small; if those units finance themselves largely from a tax, like the property tax, whose yield is heavily conditioned by the way in which land is used within each jurisdiction; if the political units have the power to control land use, then there will be an overwhelming temptation to make fiscal considerations the primary criterion of land-use controls.

Political units will seek to preserve favorable balances of revenue producers and public service consumers, and those that have unfavorable balances will seek to reverse them. In particular, all will have an interest in excluding households without above-average incomes and wealth. Clearly, this is precisely the way large numbers of suburban local governments have behaved over the past twenty years or so, and the exclusionary zoning that results has powerful impacts on the distribution of the metropolitan population and its access to employment opportunities. A direct solution (that is, simply overriding or eliminating small-unit land-use control) seems unattainable. Indirect solutions involve fiscal reforms: equalizing grants, area-wide or statewide financing (especially of the schools), and less dependence on the property tax with its close tie to the pattern of local land use.

The property tax has a bad name among fiscal reformers, and not just because of its tie to land-use controls. It is generally held to be a deterrent to housing investment and consumption on the part of renters and less affluent owner-occupants (for whom the offsetting federal income tax advantages of home ownership are of no consequence) and thus a real problem for central cities where renters and nonaffluent homeowners predominate. The residential component of the property tax is conventionally held to be steeply regressive in its incidence; it is alleged by many, including me, to be the most regressive major element in the tax system Americans confront. Because these aspects of the property tax on housing are less obnoxious the lower the level of tax, shifts of fiscal responsibility to higher levels of government that do not employ the property tax, of the types discussed in earlier paragraphs, are partial solutions, as is greater reliance by central city local governments on non-property revenue sources, such as sales and income taxation.

Also popular with reformers are income-conditioned property tax relief devices operated through state income tax machinery, devices now in operation in one form or another in 21 states (seventeen of these states instituted their programs in the past four years). Academic reformers, but not elected officials, also consider a major shift in the property tax toward heavier taxation of land values and lighter taxation of buildings a radical reform that would be highly beneficial.

Finally, a large proportion of fiscal reformers of diverse ideological persuasions consider the general failure of urban governments to employ charges for public services aggressively, for services where income-redistribution or consumption-maximizing goals are absent, an appalling defect in the fiscal system. The outstanding opportunities for deployment of high user charges are in connection with congestion and pollution, where the public purpose is or should be to encourage resource conservation and economical use of public services, rather than maximum consumption.

THE 1970s: FISCAL EASE AND STRESS

I believe that the conventional wisdom remains valid in the main, but in the past few years there have been major events and large-scale shifts in opinion that call for some reconsideration. These recent developments have worked in different directions with regard to the fiscal plight of the metropolis. The failure of welfare reform and the cutbacks in other federally financed programs directed at poverty and poor people, both of which reflect a major shift in the general climate of opinion, clearly will hurt the large cities in fiscal as well as human terms. The liberalization of Social Security benefits in the 1972 legislation will help, perhaps a good deal more than is commonly anticipated, and there is at least some prospect for federal action on health insurance — with significant effects on locally financed health expenditure — within a few years. But on the whole, the fiscal reformers' plea for a massive shift of the fiscal responsibility for income-redistributive public expenditure seems likely to be ignored in the foreseeable future. If this is the case, those urban governments that now spend large amounts of their own resources for these purposes will then continue to face real fiscal stress in an unsympathetic world.

One reason for the lack of sympathy is the fact that for most state and local governments other than the large central cities (and low-income jurisdictions in the suburbs), the fiscal climate in the 1970s may be one of ease rather than stress. This can be, and has been, exaggerated. Moynihan (1973, pp. 9–10), for example, has said that the 1970s and 1980s "are likely to be a time when it's not so bad to be mayor, and being governor might be positively pleasant." Nevertheless, the sharp increase in federal aid to state and local governments between 1965 and 1972, culminating in the enactment of revenue sharing in 1972, the slower rate of growth in population, and the decline in school enrollments, will combine to make fiscal crisis seem a thing of the past to many state govern-ments, as well as a fair number of suburban and small-city local govern-ments. But for the large central cities, poverty and its fiscal impact, con-tinued pressure on public employee compensation levels, the apparent inability to improve productivity in the provision of public services, and public disenchantment with the effectiveness of public expenditure are likely to spell continued increases in costs and a powerful reluctance to approve the fiscal measures required to cover those costs.

Another set of recent developments and opinion shifts worthy of note here concerns the role of the property tax in local government finance. While there is always a lag between reality and its perception in a period of rapid change, the lag here is somewhat startling: Almost coinci-dentally with the emergence of fiscal ease, a populist revolt about the property tax seems to have become politically significant. No doubt the tax, as a large and highly visible one (much more visible than sales and withheld income taxes), has always been highly unpopular; it now seems to be wildly unpopular. It is not easy to discern the basis for this. One element may be the very rapid recent increase in housing property values, combined with assessment reform (in numerous states) that threatens to end the usual undertaxation of owner-occupied houses compared to other types of property. When tax bills rise to reflect rising property values, governments are in effect taxing unrealized capital gains; only fiscal economists are willing to admit that unrealized capital gains do in fact make people richer and more able to pay taxes.

Whatever the cause of the populist revolt, the political response has been clear: proposals by the President and members of Congress of all persuasions to provide federally financed property tax relief and rapid adoption by state legislatures of a variety of property tax relief measures, some related to income but most not. The intellectual response also has been a predictable one: A fair number of intellectuals are now devoting themselves to a debunking exercise, designed to demonstrate that the property tax is really a pretty good tax after all (Kristol, 1972, pp. 3–11; Peterson and Solomon, 1973, pp. 60–75).

The argument essentially is that an ideal, truly uniform property tax would amount to a general tax on capital, and its sole economic effect would be to reduce the return on capital throughout the economy. Such a tax would be a highly progressive one and would not act as a deterrent to housing. The policy implication is that we should clean up the tax, mainly by improving its administration, and thereby make it the paragon it could be. Subsidiary arguments contend that even the tax we now have would be far from regressive, if only relatively modest changes were made.

This is not the place to dispute these contentions. I disagree sharply with the policy implications, although some of the theoretical and measurement points the revisionists make have intellectual validity (Netzer, 1973). State legislatures and governors still adhere to the conventional wisdom and are busily tinkering with the property tax. However, the proposals for federal action seem to have fallen flat, and the likelihood of judicial action to force school property tax reform on the constitutional grounds of equal protection has receded with the Supreme Court's decision on this in the RODRIGUEZ case in early 1973. In short, the prospects are for continued controversy and uncertainty.

Another subject of controversy and uncertainty in the urban public economy has to do with environmental protection. One can discern some signs of backlash as the social and private costs of the environmental policies adopted in the past few years become apparent. We have legislated a number of high air and water quality standards and have provided a legislative basis for truly demanding standards in regard to other environmental concerns as well. In general, the legislation calls for uniform reductions in the production of wastes or other environmental affronts, which is far from the least-cost method of achieving a given degree of environmental quality. If the standards are enforced, extremely high private and public costs — including some with obvious manpower and employment consequences — will result. The costs in the case of air quality standards will be largely private and internalized, in the form of higher motor vehicle capital and operating costs, higher fuel costs for electric power generation and space heating, and higher industrial process costs. However, for other aspects of environmental protection, the costs will be public and external, reflecting the continued refusal to impose taxes and charges that reduce the environmental affronts at their source: among producers and consumers.

Thus the combination of high water treatment standards applied uniformly and the refusal to institute stiff effluent charges will lead to very high levels of public expenditure for water treatment. Similar factors are likely to result in extremely high-cost solid waste disposal systems. One may question whether the willingness to meet these costs will in fact be present.

A RESEARCH AGENDA

Thus the public economy of the metropolis in the remainder of the 1970s seems likely to confront problems that are agreed to be both important and unresolved, in an environment that may not be conducive to major institutional change. All this suggests, as a perceptive observer said some years ago in another connection, that "the time for action has passed, it's time for another study." Less flippantly — a period in which the possibility for change is limited is one that can be exploited to learn more, as a platform for large-scale institutional change in the future and as a basis for more immediate incremental change. The most obvious metropolitan public sector issues about which we badly need to know more include the following:

(1) How can we make public expenditure more effective, in the sense of achieving the underlying goals that are sought? It is easy, albeit costly, to reduce class size, to put more police on patrol, appoint more judges, increase the supply of health professionals, and otherwise apply more inputs to the resolution of social problems. It is much more difficult to assure that the increased inputs will improve learning, public safety, health, and the like. It is possible to be mildly optimistic in this regard, because the analysis of effectiveness in public expenditure is truly in its infancy. Until recently there were no serious and systematic efforts to distinguish between input objectives and the ends of public expenditure, and to find effective means to these ends. Convention substituted for analysis.

(2) A related but somewhat distinctive question concerns productivity in the public sector in a narrower, more technical sense. It is fair to say that the conventional wisdom here has been that productivity in the service-producing sectors of the economy is inherently stagnant, despite a considerable body of evidence to the contrary. The conventional wisdom has been considerably bolstered by the writings of economic sages unwilling to be encumbered by a "tissue of facts." The reality of course is that productivity will not improve in the absence of pressures to force improvements and that the belief that productivity in the public sector cannot improve will preclude such pressures from developing. The fact is that governments do not use the best of currently available technology and methods and tend not to

be very receptive or helpful to the development of improved technology and methods. The customary local government use of computers solely as adding and checkwriting machines is an obvious example. I believe that there is enormous scope for improvement — the kind of improvement that is really not all that controversial.

(3) How can we deal with the presently utterly unresolved problem of public sector wage determination? The fact that recent salary advances in education have been relatively modest in the face of teacher strikes and widespread collective bargaining in public universities is no indication that a solution is at hand, for strikes in education are not very serious threats to the life of cities. Where the strike threat is more deadly or where the political clout of the public employee group is greater, rapid increases in compensation continue. Here we share a common experience with the other advanced democracies, none of which has really found the answer.

(4) How can we design income-redistributing mechanisms that are equitable among the benefited population, avoid "ratchet" effects at the threshold of eligibility, have a proper regard for work incentives, and have program costs that are tolerable to the majority who will be paying the freight? No doubt the failure of welfare reform and the antipathy to other antipoverty programs reflect a significant change in public attitudes on the part of the nonpoor majority. But the failures also reflect defects in program design, which in turn are evidence of how difficult it is to reconcile conflicting objectives. The problem is not solely one for the metropolis, but there is an important urban dimension to it, and not solely because of the concentration of the poor in central cities. A major difficulty in program design is whether and how to reflect geographic differences in national-scope programs; this issue includes the question of the appropriate roles of local government in policy decisions, administration, and financing.

(5) Concerning finance per se, one glaringly obvious problem is that of the truly poor city — what might be called "the Newark problem" — a jurisdiction that cannot be self-sustaining and still provide the high public service standards now expected in urban areas. Such jurisdictions occur in three forms: first, the

central city whose size is small compared to the total size of the metropolitan area or urban region in which it is located, and which thus can end up becoming a place of residence only for the region's poor and deserted by much of its economic base, like Newark, Paterson, and Gary, among others; second, the poor suburb, often largely black or Hispanic; and third, the isolated free-standing city in a declining section of a state that is generally affluent. The number of such places is not large; they are sports in the system. As sports, they are unlikely to be saved by changes in formulas for intergovernmental aid that are of general application, nor is there effective general sympathy for their plight. There is real need for research on specially tailored solutions that might conceivably be acceptable to state governments.

(6) There are some finance issues of wider geographic concern. One involves the property tax: How bad is the existing institution as it actually works in practice, particularly in the larger central cities? How effective are the reforms now being considered and implemented in removing its sting? What other modifications are called for?

(7) Another problem concerns user charges, especially those related to congestion and pollution. How can the very real opportunities for economically efficient action be fully exploited? That is, what is the design of user charges that can be made workable, under the conditions that are specific to individual cities and activities? The economics are clear enough, in general terms; the specifics are anything but clear.

(8) Governments are extraordinarily effective in creating economic rents in urban areas, especially land rents, sometimes negative but more often positive ones. They are extraordinarily inept in capturing the positive rents they have created for public use. This is true in nearly all countries, including places in which land ownership is nominally public. On both efficiency and equity grounds, this failure is a serious one. There is a real need for developing mechanisms of financing that tap existing positive economic rents, avoid the large-scale generation of new uncaptured positive rents, and also avoid the generation of negative rents, again in terms of designs that are specific to the circumstances.

This is by no means an all-inclusive research agenda; I have consciously excluded a number of issues that bear on the cities, but call for national solutions with little local differentiation. I have also deliberately excluded a few widely discussed issues that I consider bogus (like the financing of urban transportation subsidies, which becomes a real issue only if one accepts the preposterous conventional wisdom that devoting more resources to transportation is good, not bad). Nevertheless, there is more than enough to keep people busy until the time for action returns.

References

Aronson, J. Richard; and Schwartz, Eli. "Financing Public Goods and the Distribution of Population in a System of Local Governments." *National Tax Journal* (June 1973), vol. 26.

Kristol, Irving. "Of Populism and Taxes." *The Public Interest* (Summer 1972), no. 28.

Levin, Henry M. "An Analysis of the Economic Effects of the New York City Sales Tax." In *Financing Government in New York City.* New York: New York University, Graduate School of Public Administration. 1966.

Moynihan, Daniel P. " 'Peace' — Some Thoughts on the 1960s and 1970s." *The Public Interest* (Summer 1973), no. 32.

Netzer, Dick. "Federal, State, and Local Finance in a Metropolitan Context." In *Issues in Urban Economics.* Edited by Harvey S. Perloff and Lowdon Wingo, Jr. Baltimore: The Johns Hopkins Press. 1968.

————. "The Incidence of the Property Tax Revisited." *National Tax Journal* (December 1973), vol. 26.

Peterson, George E.; and Solomon, Arthur P. "Property Taxes and Populist Reform." *The Public Interest* (Winter 1973), no. 30.

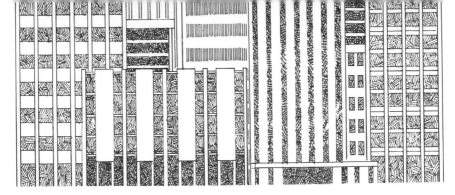

5
Problem-Oriented Manpower Research: A Management View

JAMES F. TIRONE*

In a search for a practical paradigm for manpower studies, social, political, and operational realities suggest we look with considerable suspicion on some of the hoary traditions which pass for manpower research both in business and in academe, and on some of the fictions which persist with the eternality of the common cold.

The traditions and the fictions produce circumstances which lead to wasted effort and seemingly endless research, concluding with very little that is practical to the business manager. The overriding criterion of manpower research, from a management view, is that it must lead to some useful result. This is hardly anti-intellectual. "In practical matters," as Aristotle (book X, ch. 10) said, "the end is not speculative knowledge of what is to be done, but rather the doing of it." (The precise words of the quotation will vary with translation, but the concept is pure Aristotle.)

To begin with traditions, a first casualty — we might hope — will be the platoons of labor "experts" created instanter by the wedding of the computer and the *Handbook of Labor Statistics*. As will be no news, many of us have been enamored of the "ah-hah!" phenomenon which is

* Publications director, American Telephone and Telegraph Company. While the conclusions herein are his own, the author is indebted to two colleagues for their comments and advice on the manuscript. John Falk and James Sheridan, both managers in the Human Resources Development department of AT&T were helpful with encouragement and assistance.

possible from relentless examination and manipulation of numbers. Also, statistics many times have aspects of a cultural disease in and of themselves; what William Shaw (1973, pp. 7–10) has called "a kind of snow job that buries the user." Shaw's prescription for the illness is "repeated forced feedings of perspective," which is another way of suggesting practicality.

Obviously, and as an article of scientific faith, the determination of objective reality in manpower or any other secular study is the sine qua non of good research. The "jackass fallacy" — to adopt a phrase coined by Henry Levinson (1973) in another context — is to believe that numbers per se necessarily provide a program for remedial action.

The second major problem for management in manpower research is the fiction which surrounds much of the data accumulated. As Ivar Berg (1969, pp. 115–37) has pointed out, some of us are mesmerized by our "fantasies" about people who work. These fantasies generate multiple tables as to the age distribution of the labor force, the totality of the force in year X, its presumed distribution about the United States, and so on ad infinitum. At a practical level, these data are merely interesting.

We can cope with some of those fantasies by restating some reality:

(1) The age distribution and experiential background of the work force is not material to mass employment. Tight labor circumstances, from World War II and forward to the present, have demonstrated that employers make do with or train those who are available to work. In the long run, neither of the foregoing processes has a major effect on the cost of production, assuming that there is a "long run" in the employee's association with the firm (which will be discussed subsequently).

(2) Given the dark mystery which shrouds the coming of future events, there is no rational way to know whether the anticipated numbers of people who work will be sufficient for jobs available or vice versa. That is, a Vietnam War and its demands in materiel and manpower or a massive Apollo space program and so forth are not predictable events. They profoundly affect both the locus of the demand for labor (as in the case of Apollo) and the totality of labor needed. The unpredictability of demand and location makes meaningless much of statistical trend projection as to the labor force.

(3) There are finite limits to a labor force for a given year, but the number of people available to work is vastly expandable. For

example, more married women may seek employment; vocational training of short duration may be substituted for extended college and graduate education; and we might simply remove the barrier which inhibits work by retired people whose pensions are reduced when wages reach a specified level. In short, a labor force can be very nearly the totality of the population (except, perhaps, infants and children) if a crunch comes, or if the rewards are great enough.

(4) The best evidence is that there are far more people who can be used for work than there are jobs available. The simplest demonstration of this is our development of social policy which lops off more and more of the labor force by lowering the retirement age at one end and increasing the age before which many of our young are expected to work at the other.

(5) Within some tolerable limits, even the precise location of the labor force may be unimportant. There appears to be a "shopping center" effect; the people find the market and vice versa. Curtis Harris (1973, pp. 62c–e) has pointed out: "There is an interaction between jobs and the movement of people. People do indeed follow the jobs, but there are many instances when jobs follow people, too." A classic example of the first is the "job route" of blacks migrating from the South, and the second is the influx of northerners into southern communities as industrial plants followed the sun.

(6) The work force is not a homogeneous "thing"; its members obviously differ as a function of many factors. Not the least of them is the "immigrant" factor, which characterizes much of the labor in cities in the northeastern tier of states. The consequence of the immigrant factor is that a national corporation experiences the sense of being two companies: one which exists in an intense and dangerous environment; the other nicely middle class with all its connotations and stability.

(7) The long-range effect of the Civil Rights Act and its amendments, plus the regulations of the Office of Federal Contract Compliance, will be to moot most of the artificial labor imbalances which have resulted from cultural limitations on the employment of women and minorities. The principle now is well established in the law that an employer's work force, if he or she is to defend hiring policies against charges of discrimination

and the penalties thereof, must in most cases reasonably mirror the relevant labor force seeking employment in a community. To bring that about, the Equal Employment Opportunity Commission (as of June 1973) had filed more than 120 law-suits against employers, some of them the foremost corporations in the nation (*U.S. News and World Report*, 1973, pp. 88–90). (AT&T had already reached a settlement with government agencies as to minorities and women and many aspects of employment.)

(8) Finally, aggregates such as the "work force of the United States" and the mean, mode, standard deviation, regression coefficient, and so forth, are relatively meaningless at the facility level where the labor force is in fact employed. This is not to say that gross measures and residuals thereof should therefore be abandoned, but simply a statement of fact that the convenient tools of gross analysis say nothing about the *actual* labor force that will be willing to accept employment at the going wage on the manager's premises. There is some evidence that the social factors in employment may have more to do with the actual applicants a firm received than the labor force in a community would suggest ("Worker Alienation, 1972," 1973).

All of the foregoing have the consequence of delimiting the areas in which labor force research may be said to be genuinely problem oriented or pragmatic. Such a program of study may usefully begin from an understanding of employer experience in:

(1) Employment of people

(2) Retention of people

(3) Jobs, people, and motivation

Analysis of the first three points should lead us to a fourth: some avenues for research.

EMPLOYMENT OF PEOPLE

The ability of a company to attract workers for employment is obviously a function of the firm's recruiting practices, reputation, working conditions, salary policy, treatment of employees, and so forth. There are also external.factors (e.g., unemployment rate, cultural appropriateness of the work offered, and so on) over which the employer seldom has control. A common sense approach should suggest that there ought to be some definable relationship among these factors.

Proving that relationship is another matter; first, because the variables are so confounded with each other that isolating them for manipulation and study is almost impossible. The employee seems to respond to a gestalt wherein the whole results from an intermixture of the various elements on a personal level. Second, the corporation itself changes the relationship among the internal and external factors in employment by varying the conditions of employment (e.g., abandoning the requirement of a high school diploma).

In any case, the Bell Telephone Company experience has been that the unemployment rate has not seriously affected the total numbers of employees hired (Table 7), although the rate may have had other effects. It is reasonable to assume that employment offices had difficulty in hiring people and that these difficulties fluctuated over the years. It may also be true that Bell's demand is indicative of other demand, and hence the unemployment rate went down. But it is also clear from the evidence that the labor pool *available* for employment changes vastly as a function of employer decisions.

TABLE 7

Bell Telephone Company Employment and
National Unemployment Rates
(1960–72)

Year	Bell Telephone Company New Hires (thousands)	U.S. Average Unemployment Rate
1960	77.3	5.5%
1961	60.8	6.7
1962	73.7	5.5
1963	86.7	5.7
1964	97.6	5.2
1965	115.4	4.5
1966	162.1	3.8
1967	135.4	3.8
1968	160.8	3.6
1969	215.9	3.5
1970	191.6	4.9
1971	108.2	5.9
1972	79.5	5.6

One clear example of this is in metropolitan areas. Table 8 indicates how Bell companies enlarged their work force in 1971 by increasing employment of nonwhites (the surge of minority employees shows, in fact, from 1968). As social and cultural limitations on employment faded, the result was a vast enlargement of the available labor force. Also, major change in the labor pool occurred which cannot be demonstrated statistically.

Historically, employment by major firms has tended to reflect the mores and standards of the middle classes, particularly those of the midwestern small town. High standards of demeanor, dress, and appear-

TABLE 8

Nonwhite Employment by Bell Telephone Companies
(1971)

Company	Nonwhites as a Percentage of Total Hires	Nonwhites as a Percentage of Working-Age Population*
New England	6.2%	2.8%
Southern New England	22.1	6.0
New York	30.1	12.9
New Jersey	17.8	10.5
Pennsylvania	23.4	8.7
C & P	31.8	18.8
Southern	15.0	19.8
South Central	23.7	19.3
Ohio	20.2	9.0
Michigan	22.4	11.4
Indiana	13.3	6.6
Wisconsin	9.1	3.3
Illinois	27.1	12.7
Northwestern	6.4	2.1
Southwestern	19.5	10.9
Mountain	8.9	5.1
Pacific N.W.	17.7	3.9
Pacific	19.5	10.6
TOTAL, Bell companies	20.0	11.4

* Taken from Bureau of the Census, U.S. Department of Commerce, *General Population Characteristics, United States Summary, 1970* (Washington, D.C.: U.S. Government Printing Office, 1970), Table 62.

ance were expected of candidates for employment. No one needed instruction as to these requirements, and indeed many managers would have been surprised to learn that any other standards were reasonable. The dress and manners revolution of the 1960s forced a conflict upon managers: They could accept employees with beards, blue jeans, brightly hued shirts, women in slacks and sweaters, and so forth, or they would do with a vastly limited labor force. The bending of cultural rules could be heard from coast to coast. Furthermore, life-styles as to work required adaptation to large numbers in the work force who preferred part-time employment.

There are of course costs associated with a conscious attempt to enlarge the pool of available labor. More effort is required to attract people, and very likely, a broad hiring policy requires interviewing more people to employ a lesser percentage of them, since the absolute number of employees needed may not have increased. In 1970, to attract 917,000 applicants in 27 cities cost Bell companies $15.72 per applicant; the cost per person hired was $156.82. Total expenses were:

Expense	Amount
Advertising	$ 2,587,654
Salary	10,083,262
Other	1,745,531
TOTAL	$14,416,447

In brief, an employer may increase sizably the work force from which he may draw in almost any metropolitan area by variations in his expectations and work rules. If the firm will accept women as well as men in all occupations; people, irrespective of color or national origin; performance rather than diplomas; part-time as well as full-time labor; and many other adaptations, the available work force expands considerably. Such expansion may limit the need for research. (It ought not be necessary to say "all other factors being equal." That is, an employer who operates a sweat shop on the borderline of the minimum wage, and with a community history of human degradation, is going to have a difficult order increasing his or her labor force under almost any conditions.)

RETENTION OF PEOPLE

As we have seen, the largest employers very likely may determine for themselves how large or how small the labor pool shall be in an area at a given point. Sufficient labor may be attracted as a function of many variables and their manipulation. That different employment costs attach to different strata of labor seems reasonable. A newspaper ad for engineers with specific training and experience will bring a reasonable sample of replies; a similar ad for telephone operators may not even reach into the community from which the employer hopes to draw some of that force. Indeed, employment devices in some cities have called for ingenuity rather than conventional methods.

To recruit minority personnel in 31 cities in 1970, Bell companies employed multiple strategies. Some of them were:

Activity	Number
Ads in newspapers with significant minority readership	847
Ads on radio stations with significant minority listeners	3,446
Recruiting programs at high schools with significant minority enrollment	4,892
Workshops for guidance counselors about Bell jobs	57
"Job fairs"	66
Cities in which telephone companies had Saturday training programs for high school students	12

The totality of the functions necessary simply to obtain applicants adds significantly to the costs of operation in cities.

Beyond these differences in employment costs, the more significant factor in the employment of entry labor is training cost. While it is true that in some industries the division of labor has developed so greatly that training costs are negligible, a great many other firms find training, sometimes quite extended, essential ("Worker Alienation, 1972," 1973). This becomes more time consuming, and hence more expensive, where reading levels have declined among the work force in a central city over a decade or so, or where cultural patterns have vastly changed. Now the employer — for reasons which may range from enlarging the labor pool to meeting goals for equal employment — finds that he or she must engage in basic education as well as training.

In the telephone industry, training tends to be extensive because specific skills required are not part of school curricula. In a major city in 1971, the average cost of training for a telephone operator was $548; $1,910 for a business office representative; $240 for one basic craft job (frame person). To this of course should be added the employment cost of $157.

We might assume that the cost of such employment and training should be prorated over some term of employment. What is a "reasonable term" is open to argument; but for purpose of analysis, let us say three years to recover initial employment and training costs — or $705 for the telephone operator ($548 plus $157).

The consequence of this kind of analysis is that one may begin to calculate the cost of short-term force loss. For example, if the operator left after one year, the cost of the loss could be the remaining two years, or $470. If resignation occurs after two years, then $235 would be the true cost of the premature loss of that person. After three years, we might assume that the cost of employment and training were depreciated.

It is plain from these elementary numbers that the cost of employment and training can be negligible per person *if* the time span for recovery (i.e., period of employment) is a function of the initial cost. For example, if the employee cost $3,000 to put to work, then we might say three years for full recovery; if $6,000, then six years. Admittedly, that is a simplified mode of analysis; in fact, we might want to attach varying percentages to the year of resignation and the costs thereto.

Briefly, in sophisticated industries requiring more than minimal training, the crucial factor in cost is not in employment or even training, but rather it is a function of the time span in which the employee remains with the firm. As has been mentioned, the arguable point is the reasonable term for depreciation of the employment training charges — and in some respects such discussion is meaningless. The reason for this denigration of the argument is plain as one observes the means by which depreciation is derived for some machinery—many times by "guts and a guess," as one engineer put it. In other words, there is no doubt that reasonable people could arrive at a reasonable term of time for the depreciation of the cost of employment and training.

Why all this concern about defining these costs? Because by arriving at cost figures and conclusions as to amortization, we have in fact attached a measurement device to the effective retention of people on the payroll. Such specificity is an important achievement and is also a contribution because it quantifies what hitherto has been unmeasurable in that all manner of causation might be associated with force loss. The uses of the measure are plain. A manager frequently is evaluated in relation to a specific set of standards, with precise numbers attached, when it comes to the preservation of the firm's assets or, in the instance of sales people, in goods sold as a percentage of some goal. Unless he or she is absolutely intransigent in the management of people, the manager seldom experiences a negative consequence in his or her career from force loss, even if platoons of people wander through the facility.

People who have worked in factories or their equivalent will have their own tales of "man's inhumanity to man," but a recent example from the press will illustrate what is believed to be a not infrequent intransigence. In an auto plant recently, two disgruntled workers, shielded by sympathizing fellow workers, locked themselves into a power cage and shut down an assembly line, idling about 4,500 workers. The goal of all this was to protest an "abusive and abrasive" superintendent. After eleven hours of negotiation between the higher management and the two men, the superintendent was discharged, and the assembly line returned to production (New York *Times*, July 25, 1973).

This is an extreme example of conflict, and experience would suggest that employees and managers at all levels resolve analagous conflicts with much less direct confrontation. The incident does illustrate how easy it is for a higher level of management genuinely not to know what is taking place in the relationships between supervisors and employees. Yet it can be demonstrated in sophisticated industries, where some training is required before effective production, that the costs of production increase as a condition of considerable short-term employment. It is therefore to the interest of a management to determine whether its particular force loss is a function of societal factors or whether such loss is fomented and indeed encouraged in subtle ways by first-level supervision. There is some evidence that the interaction between employees and supervisors accounts for about a third of employee resignations.

In a private study conducted for a Bell company, 166 out of 206 employees who had resigned from a single telephone district in an eighteen-month period were interviewed as to reasons for quitting. The results demonstrated a constellation of reasons for leaving employment — and they may be categorized as a lack of personal satisfaction, supervisor and job pressures, perception of future employment, and other reasons. Within that data, 38 percent included treatment by supervisors as "very or fairly important" in their particular constellation of reasons. To have that force loss measurable and assignable ought to result in a significant reduction in resignations and hence a lowering of employment and training costs.

Having been somewhat hard-nosed in assigning causation as to resignations, we are in fairness compelled to point out that force loss cannot totally be charged to managers. Other factors — social, psychological, and cultural — contribute to resignations of people from jobs. It should be possible, however, to establish over time a norm as to resignation levels for a facility, estimate a range for fluctuation on a seasonal or other basis, and ascribe to the mode of management those resignations for which we cannot otherwise account. However, this is a lot more simply said than done, and we shall return to this as we look down the avenues for research in metropolitan manpower subsequently.

Jobs, People, and Motivation

Beyond costs, this concern with retention of employees in a sophisticated corporation is a reflection of a long-term trend in the history of human labor. Under other circumstances, Weiner (1954) argued for a "human use of human beings," and some of the experience of the last fifty years (at least) suggests that is exactly where we are headed. This humanization has been accomplished by a continuous stream of legislation, incorporating into law over time the nation's sense of what was fair and reasonable. Beginning with the Railway Labor Act of 1926, a series of statutes and administrative regulations has sought to define and normalize relationships between employees and employers. This body of basic labor law has been supplemented with the Social Security Act, Fair Labor Standards Act, Civil Rights Act, the Equal Pay Act, and the Manpower Development and Training Act — each protective of the employee in some aspect of work.

We shall assert also that the recent obsession with "blue-collar blues" and "white-collar woes" is part of that trend toward humanization. Other aspects include worker motivation, job enrichment, adapting jobs to people, and so on — a sociology of labor which frequently takes on social worker overtones. However tangentially, these developments also relate to the recognition that retention of a trained force has economic value.

A preliminary to embracing the analysis of blues and woes and various nostrums ought to be a simple look at the data. Table 9 illustrates the change in employment structure in the United States in the half-century 1920 to 1970. Aside from the major shift of employment from production to services, the data show a sizable decline in manufacturing as a percentage of total employees — roughly from more than a third in 1920

TABLE 9

Nonagricultural Employees, by Industry Division
(1920 and 1970)

Industry	1920		1970	
	Number*	Percent	Number*	Percent
Mining	1,239	4.53	622	0.88
Construction	848	3.10	3,347	4.74
Manufacturing	10,658	38.97	19,393	27.44
Transportation and public utilities	3,998	14.62	4,498	6.37
Wholesale and retail trade**	4,467	16.33	14,950	21.16
Finance, insurance and real estate**	1,111	4.06	3,679	5.21
Services**	2,363	8.64	11,577	16.38
Government**	2,603	9.52	12,597	17.93
TOTAL	27,350	100.00	70,664	100.00

* In thousands.
** Combined percentages in these four areas were 38.55 in 1920 and 60.58 in 1970.
SOURCE: Bureau of Labor Statistics, U.S. Department of Labor, *Handbook of Labor Statistics* (Washington, D.C.: U.S. Government Printing Office, 1971), p. 80.

to about a fourth in 1970. Furthermore, economists of the Morgan Guaranty Company (1973) estimate that less than 2 percent of the work force is employed on assembly lines. That would approximate one and a half million people (1970 basis) — not a negligible number of people, but certainly not a basis for media hysteria about blue-collar blues. In addition, the premise that vast numbers of people are dissatisfied with their jobs has some rough sledding when it scrapes against other information. A Gallup poll in early 1973 reported that among a national sample of respondents, 11 percent admitted to work dissatisfaction (New York *Times*, March 27, 1973, p. 22).

The villains at work in creating dissatisfaction are alleged to be large organizations and technology. "Supposedly," as Kaplan (1973, pp. 46–48) has pointed out, "the reduced diversity and routinization of the workplace have increased the malaise among American workers." Although his evidence is too lengthy to review here, Kaplan's summary of the research findings as to this villainy is useful:

(1) Workers desire more control in their work routines but still expect managers to manage.

(2) While there are pockets of job dissatisfaction, most workers are satisfied with their work.

(3) Job complexity has an effect on psychological functioning, but the perception and interpretation of the complexity is idiosyncratic (Kahn *et al.*, 1964).*

(4) Men employed in bureaucratic organizations tend to be more intellectually flexible, open to new experience, self-directed as to values, and with greater self-esteem than men who work in nonbureaucratic organizations.

(5) There is little evidence that negative work experiences are carried beyond the workplace and generalized into feelings of alienation and anomie.

Despite the evidence, a new industry has been dedicated to social work among employees. It comes disguised in assorted terminology, and usually put forth as though it were Gospel According to Herzberg (as Freud protested that he was not a Freudian, no doubt Herzberg would protest that he is not a Herzbergian). This has evoked angry responses.

An industrial engineer argues in 60 point type in one publication that "Job Enrichment Is a Fraud" (*Boardroom Report*, 1973, pp. 7–8). Winpisinger (1972), general vice president of the International Association of Machinists and Aerospace Workers (AFL-CIO), proposes: "If you want to enrich the job, enrich the paycheck. The better the wage, the greater the job satisfaction. There is no better cure for the 'blue-collar blues.'"

In the absence of controls and sequential manipulation of variables, the "research" of job enrichment sounds more like evangelical testimony than scientific psychology. Hulin and Blood (1968, pp. 41–55), Lawler (1969, pp. 426–35), and Bishop and Hill (1971, pp. 175–81) have raised serious issues about job enrichment theories as panaceas for the evils asserted to result from modern work. While the Bishop and Hill research is *not* generalizable because of the subjects used, the evidence did suggest that under those circumstances a reasonable explanation for

---

* An excellent summary of manifestations of stress, a subject which has since generated a good deal of study.

changes produced by job manipulation could be the Hawthorne effect (the data are more complex than has been outlined; those interested, see Homans, 1962, in the references). To complete the jeremiad, Sales (1969, pp. 325–36) reviews a panorama of medical literature suggesting that organizational role — particularly role overload, such as might result from job enrichment in some instances — is a "significant risk factor" in the incidence of coronary disease. In simulation of role overload in laboratory settings, Sales found that high workloads "may have strong, diverse, and pervasive effects upon individuals exposed to them, and that some of these effects may be observed in biochemical and physiological variables known to be related to health" (1970, pp. 592–608). He argues for an "appropriate matching of individuals to environments" to reduce the stress factors.

This devil's advocacy is not by any means the entire story. Levitan and Johnston (1973, pp. 35–41) have put forward a reasonable and rational analysis of the utility of job redesign and have urged innovations that "represent the wishes of workers" (rather than those of productivity-minded managers or well-intentioned consultants). In my view, a manager has an obligation to the shareowners to institute those reasonable innovations which will maximize the investment, and the innovations certainly include job restructuring where that seems to contribute to the bottom line of the balance sheet. But as Levitan and Johnston also suggest, neither the manager nor the rest of the workers ought to see job redesign or enrichment as a step into the Promised Land. The step may be common sense sometimes and maybe, but nothing more.

Let us go one step farther. Serious question, simply on the basis of the evidence, must arise as to whether a sociology of work even needs a condescending language of "enrichment" to describe what is occurring when managements intervene in how work is conducted, and thus indicate their interest therein. Roethlisberger and Dickson (1939) and their studies at the Western Electric works at Hawthorne require rediscovery, and there is every reason to believe theirs is a more parsimonious explanation of what changes worker production than the mushy literature which has since emerged.

It is interesting to note that the Western Electric Company planned for 1974 a year-long observance of the fiftieth anniversary of the Hawthorne studies. "The conclusion" (of the studies), an AT&T management report (1973, p. 3) says, "was that the attitude of management, as reflected in the changes introduced, had changed the attitude *and the output* of the women more than had the changes in work conditions themselves" (italics added). Please note two points: management and change. They shall be referred to in the next section as "planned variation."

SOME AVENUES FOR MANPOWER RESEARCH

All of the foregoing may be said to be prologue, the conditions precedent to problem-oriented manpower research. Before some specific research directions are outlined, it may be useful to summarize what has been said:

(1) Managers require the disaggregation of labor statistics, gathering them at the geographic level from which the plant facility will draw its manpower.

(2) There are fundamental differences between the labor force that is recruited *within* a central city and that which is attracted in a satellite or suburban community.

(3) Employers, within the bounds of the law, in fact define their own work force, and this is expandable and contractible as a function of employer requirements, although different costs attach to the decisions reached.

(4) Establishments whose work compels sizable investment in training, making highly economic the retention of labor, require a set of concrete measures so that the causation of force loss may be determined.

(5) It is demonstrable in law, and otherwise, that humanization of the conditions of work has been taking place for at least a half-century, and the evidence is miniscule yet supportive of the belief that there is a large-scale worker dissatisfaction or that a secular religion of work is truly useful.

The proposals below grow in part from the summary and will include some research experiences of the American Telephone & Telegraph Company in those directions.

Labor Market Forecasting

Manpower aspects in locating a firm's facilities usually involve both determining where the labor is and then calculating a site that maximizes availability to that labor. But the critical point is: What *part* of that labor will in fact go to work for the firm? In other words, if the jobs offered are likely to be attractive to people from lower income groups whose education has ended at the high school level, then there isn't much sense in consciously locating the facility in a high-income community where 90 percent or more of the youngsters are going directly into college after high school.

As a class, these younger age groups — let us say, eighteen through twenty — may be termed "entry" labor, relatively untrained for any specific work and seeking employment which provides training and opportunity, or at least experience translatable into other employment elsewhere. Telephone companies have over the years had large numbers of entry-type jobs that have been seen as offering opportunities. But in the late 1960s these companies began to find that entry labor was more likely to be found in the central city than in suburban communities.

The figure which follows is a fairly typical finding; it represents an SMSA, with the central city at the center of the drawing, and depicts study findings about the percentage of the total female labor force in each municipality that was *not* going to college after high school and hence would be available for entry work. Other data showed that the percentages were not significantly different for males. As the figure plainly shows, the data strongly suggested locating new facilities in the central city if a company held to the strategy of hiring younger people as entry labor. Obviously a change of strategy might dictate other studies and other conclusions (and such a change had occurred in many companies).

In any case, a sizable portion (about a fourth) of the Bell System labor already was in central cities, a vast number of Bell customers is there, and it was plain that irrespective of age-hire decisions for entry jobs, some way would have to be found to attract labor to Bell employment within the central city.

Similar labor studies being conducted by Hugh Folk of the University of Illinois suggested that there might be some mutuality of interest in manpower problems in a central city. In cooperation with the Illinois Bell Company and AT&T, Dr. Folk and his associates developed what came to be called the Community Labor Market Information System, or COLMIS.

COLMIS calls for three "inputs": a new hire sample, a nonhire sample, and relating the data to "community areas." A systemic coding of the data also was called for. The outputs of the study are: a new hire rate analysis, an "import-export" analysis, and a nonhire analysis. The final application of all of the foregoing is the use of COLMIS in manage-

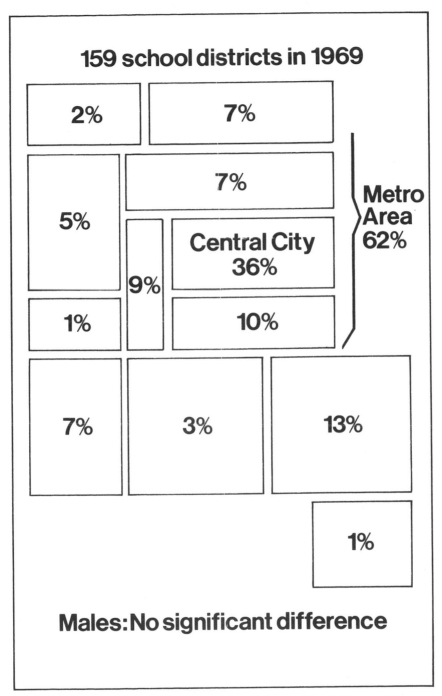

Female High School Graduates Available to Work Near a City

ment decision making. A look at each of the parts will permit an understanding of the whole of the system. Also, COLMIS was constructed with data from the city of Chicago and all specifics that follow (employees, community areas, and so forth) will be in terms of that city.

New Hire Sample

An unstated premise of COLMIS is that the demographic characteristics of the employees a firm now is hiring will be similar on the average to the characteristics of the employees the firm is *most likely* to get in the near future. Thus the first problem is to determine accurately for each occupational group the characteristics of the employees in fact being hired, and a sampling technique among new hires (*not* total employees) was developed to permit such identification. (COLMIS also was conceived as a dynamic system, such that a periodic new-hire sample would validate the premise.)

Nonhire Sample

A similar process of sampling and identification of characteristics was carried out among the records of people who had applied for employment and who were, for some reason, unwilling or unable to complete the route to a job. The specific reason for nonemployment was a part of these data.

Coding the Data

For both samples, 28 variables (as applicable) were collected, including such data as: the area of the city in which the person lived; the job sought; locus of the job sought; the person's sex, color, education, labor force status (unemployed?), and so forth. A standardized system of reporting was developed.

Community Data Base

The city of Chicago is made up of 75 distinct community areas, from number 1, which is Rogers Park on the far north side, to number 75, which is Morgan Park on the south. Where a city has a similar community system, the use of COLMIS is simplified. However, it may be necessary to "construct communities," and these *should be aggregated from census tract units*. The units are the foundation of the community data base. Sources of additional information might be health and vital statistics gathered by a city.

From the census tracts, seventy variables are collected for each community (real or constructed). These include such standbys as: total population; males and females by age, sex, and color; education levels;

housing units; and so on. Instructions also are included in the COLMIS material for updating the information or adding additional variables from other sources.

New Hire Rate Analysis

Data from the new hire sample first of all enable us to relate hires to community area and assign a "new hire rate" (i.e., hires as a percentage of total labor available) to each community. The community data base, at the same time, provides us with information about manpower and its dimensions in each tract.

In addition, as will have occurred to some readers, the total data collected permit regression analysis to identify which community variables associate with the highest likelihood of employment. In Chicago in 1970, the variables that most closely associated with hires were as follows:

(1) Percentage of nonwhites (birth and population), which represented the presence of a population group which found telephone company jobs attractive and was marked by high "immigration" from southern communities

(2) Percentage of males in the community, which was believed to be a measure of the social stability of the community and hence acceptance of work as a goal or norm

(3) Level of education, which showed that high school students sought telephone entry employment, but that the regression coefficient was negative when college education at some level took place

Finally, the new hire sample and community data base permitted some analysis by simple descriptive statistics which, while they may not be elegant, turned out to be very useful.

Nonhire Analysis

This information tells the firm quite accurately who were not hired, their demographic characteristics, and the reason for nonemployment. There developed also the interesting concept of considering the nonhires as a potential pool of labor, whose members might be called on relatively easily for employment as circumstances changed.

Import-Export Analysis

COLMIS made it possible to classify each community either as an *exporter* of labor (that is, an area which contributed more hires than required by the work facility in it), or as an *importer* of labor (an area which employed more workers than the area generated). Table 10 provides an import-export analysis for a sample of the 75 communities in Chicago as experienced by the Illinois Bell Company in 1970.

The Decision Process

For each community, it is possible to arrive at the hire rate, the non-hire rate (and hence, labor reserve), and an import-export rate. These quantitative and some qualitative data (availability of mass transportation and the like) made it possible for the company to focus on seven community areas in Chicago that indicated a labor market potential encouraging to facility installation or expansion.

TABLE 10

Import-Export Analysis of Telephone Employees in
Selected Chicago Communities
(1970)

Community Area	Number of Traffic Employees		Net Import-Export*
	Required in Community Area	Residing in Community Area	
Rogers Park	19	40	+21
West Ridge			
Uptown	43	20	−23
Lincoln Square		20	+20
North Center			
Lakeview	25	20	− 5
Lincoln Park		10	+10
Near North Side		30	+30
Edison Park			
Norwood Park		10	+10
Jefferson Park			
Forest Glen			
North Park			
Albany Park		10	+10
Portage Park			

* Plus symbol (+) indicates that the community *exports* employees; minus symbol (−) indicates that the community *imports* employees.

COLMIS *in an Unknown Community*

While COLMIS was designed to cope with the expansion of telephone company facilities from already established bases, there remained the possibility that installations would be required in areas where the company had no previous labor experience. A section of the COLMIS instructional manual provided for this contingency.

Briefly, the proposal suggested identifying certain variables which might be expected on theoretical grounds to associate with typical employment in the Bell System and then, by regression analysis, arriving at a statistical ranking of the communities examined. A formula was derived for calculating a new hire rate in a statistical manner, using regression and census data from known communities.

These procedures for the "unknown communities" raised considerable doubt. Some managers felt that this was too theoretical an approach — and for all practical purposes that ends the matter, because one is not likely to find managers willing to make heavy investments of money in new facilities on the basis of theory and statistics alone.

In summary, COLMIS was a brilliant approach to estimating available labor in a central city and its contiguous areas, but seemed a little risky to use elsewhere. This would suggest some rigorous study as to how COLMIS might be revised so that it could be extended to areas where a firm has no labor experience, and in such a way that probabilities of accuracy might be attached to the data.

"Immigrant" Labor

This section is meant to apply to manpower which may be said to be "immigrant" to the city. The word "immigrant" is descriptive, not pejorative. Our cities, some more than others, historically have been the educational sites for newcomers to the labor market, followed by entry into the middle class and the movement to the suburbs. Congressman Herman Badillo (Democrat, New York) has pointed out that this "traditional process has come to an end," or at the very least has become difficult to achieve, and unless we can find ways to reactivate the mechanism "we will not have a city but a vast poverty neighborhood" (New York *Times*, August 9, 1973, p. 34). This kind of neighborhood universally produces educational defects, adverse life-styles, and all of the ills the poor are prey to throughout the world, irrespective of sex, color, or language.

The consequence for employers is that they find in central cities fewer people to hire who *already* are fully prepared to take a place in the labor market. The work which has a foreseeable future demands facility with language, appropriateness of dress, communicative skills, behavior within certain parameters, and in many instances familiarity with the geography of the city. Most of this may be summed under "cultural skills," with many employers assuming that applicants had learned them prior to employment. Without such learning, applicants are likely to be turned away by the gatekeepers. Experience also has taught many employers that the absence of these cultural skills need not be a bar to employment.

One Bell company experimented briefly with what was known as an "employment-training-retention" center in a central city. A series of economic and business circumstances prevented obtaining data that were not confounded by other factors, but the principle of the center is worth rescuing. The concept was that it should be possible to bring people into a large company and that they could obtain culturally appropriate work and behavior rather quickly by direct communication of information, rather than waiting until they learned it through their pores. A supposition was that such a process of employment and training ought to result in a higher retention rate. What is required is a relatively simple demonstration, with unconfounded and clear-cut results, as to whether such orientation can be achieved in a relatively inexpensive way and with such documentation that illustrates workable, rather than social worker approaches.

Planned Variation

In this chapter, the phrase "planned variation" refers to conscious efforts to bring about changes in the work people do. The best psychological and work evidence says, I think, that the interest of others in what one does, and *sometimes* changes in the work one does, affects both production and how people feel about themselves and their work. (Two psychological constructs might be said to be operative: approval by the reference or a significant other group as reinforcement, and variety as an antidote to boredom as a practice effect.) The human robots, as Sheppard and Herrick (1972) suggest, may disappear as younger workers protest inhumanities in the system and as technology advances. We are beginning to see the gradual introduction of robots into some manufacturing processes, but it is doubtful that the tedious and dirty work of the world is going to disappear tomorrow (Rosenblatt, 1973, pp. 93–104).

As pointed out earlier, we run the risk of being accused of manipulation of people if we try to advance an evangelical view of work. The alternative is for managers to advance change in such a way that the interests of all parties thereto are preserved; for example, the interest of managers. We have reached the point in our society where a firm runs genuine risks where its managers are undirectional, so fixated on results that they have lost sight of how to organize the work about them to the extent that they actually demonstrate their interest in the people who are working.

As to change — it is not solely a managerial prerogative. There is every logic in the world to the rationalization of work, the restructuring of jobs where this seems reasonable and practicable. But the change referred to here is whether employee *A* shall be a clerk or a semiskilled craftsman, on a job inside the plant or outside, and so forth. In other words, how shall we give the human beings maximum feasible control over their work lives while at the same time we maintain the necessities of production?

One device now being used by Bell companies is an "upgrade and transfer bureau," in which an employee initiates his or her own application for transfer to other work or to a job graded higher on the career ladder. It is too soon to measure the results of this process, but certainly the attempt is being made to hand back to the employee more control over what work he or she will do.

In any case, a practicable direction of manpower research would be to determine carefully whether planned variation and its components produce some measurable results demonstrably useful to the firm and its people; also to determine whether all people genuinely want change in their work lives. Perhaps we must accept the possibility that some truly fine people live a carefully circumscribed existence in which change is a catastrophe and not a stimulus.

Organizational Diversity

Bennis (1966, p. ix), after a year attempting to be president of the University of Cincinnati, concluded that "a viable managerial strategy does not lie in consensus." The function of managers is to manage; that is their *raison d'être*. The authority and responsibility for decisions are not shared. Nothing said here is meant to be opposite to that principle.

How one manages is another matter. The simplest observable fact is that all styles of management work in the hands of some people at different times, and with different tradeoffs. Yet it is also observable that all styles of management and modes of work do not maximize the interests and potentialities of all people. (It is true that there is not much to maximize on a production line, but as has been pointed out, not many of us are tied to mass production.)

Many corporations have attempted to cope with this maximization of work modality by various decisions — the four-day, forty-hour week, flextime, "guest" workers (i.e., people imported from other nations to do some jobs), part-time positions, second careers, and so forth. All of this is part of a developing belief that a lock-step pattern of work is going to be less and less viable in a society where large numbers of people can exist on some level without working eight hours a day, five days a week.

In brief, there is every evidence of a need for organizational diversity — a need for organizations which incorporate large numbers of people who want to work in a structured way, and others who also want to work but perhaps in a manner which takes account of various trends and tendencies, even if they are so prosaic as diurnal rhythms. Some personal experience with both types of organizations suggests great caution where the two factions have to interrelate in their work. Considerable research and experience are required before such diversity can be tolerated in a large administrative organization.

CONCLUSION

The thrust of this chapter has been to argue for reality and a practical description of issues in manpower research. We have pointed to four broad areas for research: labor force forecasting at the facility level, the transition from immigrant to more experienced labor, planned variation as a mode of employee retention, and the possibilities of organizational diversity to enable a firm to cope with developing life-styles.

With this pragmatic orientation, I hope it is also clear that we must always have broad theoretics which give rise to multiple directions for research of whatever kind. Nothing said here is intended to contradict that need for diversity; this chapter has addressed itself to one dimension of manpower study. Whatever the research conducted, however, one comes ultimately to Aristotle's admonition: Doing, and not speculation, is the goal in practical matters.

REFERENCES

Aristotle. *Nicomachean Ethics.* Book X, chapter 10.

AT&T Management Report. "Western Electric to Observe Anniversary of Hawthorne Studies." August 16, 1973 (no. 34).

Bennis, Warren. *Beyond Bureaucracy.* New York: McGraw-Hill Book Company. 1966.

Berg, Ivar E. "Education and Work." In *Manpower Strategy for the Metropolis.* Edited by Eli Ginzberg. New York: Columbia University Press. 1969.

Bishop, Ronald C.; and Hill, James W. "Effects of Job Enlargement and Job Change on Continuous but Nonmanipulated Jobs as a Function of Workers' Status." *Journal of Applied Psychology* (1971), no. 55.

Boardroom Reports. "Job Enrichment Is a Fraud." August 15, 1973.

Harris, Curtis. "The Industrial Shift South That Never Stops." *Business Week* (July 14, 1973).

Hodge, Robert W.; Siegel, Paul M.; and Rossi, Peter H. "Occupational Prestige in the United States, 1925–1963." In Reinhard Bendix and Seymour Lipset, *Class, Status and Power* (2d ed.). New York: The Free Press. 1966.

Homans, George D. *Sentiments and Activities.* New York: The Free Press. 1962.

Hulan, C. L.; and Blood, M. R. "Job Enlargement, Individual Differences and Worker Responses." *Psychological Bulletin* (1968), no. 69.

Kahn, R. L.; *et al. Organizational Stress.* New York: John Wiley. 1964.

Kaplan, H. Roy. "How *Do* Workers View Their Work in America?" *Monthly Labor Review* (June 1973).

Lawler, E. E. "Job Design and Employee Motivation." *Personnel Psychology* (1969), no. 22.

Levinson, Henry. *The Great Jackass Fallacy.* Boston: Harvard University. 1973.

Levitan, Sar A.; and Johnston, William B. "Job Redesign, Reform, Enrichment — Exploring the Limitation." *Monthly Labor Review* (July 1973).

Morgan Guaranty Trust Company, New York. "Mouseville's Blue Collar Blues." *Morgan Guaranty Survey* (March 1973).

New York *Times*. March 27, 1973.

—————. "On 'Building Walls around the Middle Class.' " August 9, 1973. (Letters.)

—————. "Two Workers Lock Themselves in Cage and Halt Assembly Line." July 25, 1973.

Roethlisberger, F. J.; and Dickson, W. J. *Management and the Worker — An Account of a Research Program Conducted by the Western Electric Company, Chicago.* Cambridge, Massachusetts: Harvard University Press. 1939.

Rosenblatt, Alfred. "Robots Handling More Jobs on Industrial Assembly Lines." *Electronics* (July 19, 1973).

Sales, Stephen M. "Organizational Role as a Risk Factor in Coronary Disease." *Administrative Science Quarterly* (September 1969).

—————. "Some Effects of Role Overload and Role Underload." *Organizational Behavior and Human Performance* (1970), no. 5.

Shaw, William H. "Paradoxes, Problems and Progress." *Journal of the American Statistical Association* (March 1973).

Sheppard, Harold L.; and Herrick, Neal Q. *Where Have All the Robots Gone? Worker Dissatisfaction in the 70's.* New York: The Free Press. 1972.

U.S. *News and World Report.* "Impact of Spreading Crackdown on Job Bias." June 18, 1973.

Wiener, Norbert. *The Human Use of Human Beings.* Garden City, New York: Doubleday, Anchor Books. 1954.

Winpisinger, William. "Job Enrichment, Another Part of the Forest." *Proceedings of the 25th Annual Meeting of the Industrial Relations Research Association*, Madison, Wisconsin, 1972.

"Worker Alienation, 1972." Hearings before the U.S. Senate Subcommittee on Employment, Manpower and Poverty, July 25 and 26, 1973. Washington, D.C.: U.S. Government Printing Office. 1973.

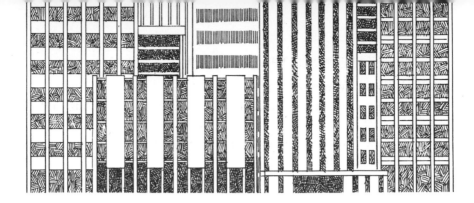

6
Minorities and the City

THOMAS SOWELL*

American ethnic minorities have long been identified with the city, although Scandinavian and German immigrants sought farmland, the Scots-Irish sought the frontier, and — until after World War I — American blacks were overwhelmingly rural. Perhaps it is not so much the history as the *progress* of American ethnic groups which has been bound up with urbanization. The most striking "success" group among the American minorities — the Jews — were urbanized centuries before they came to America. The minorities most often described as "disadvantaged" — blacks, chicanos, Puerto Rican migrants — are all relative newcomers to the city. Harlem, the oldest metropolitan black ghetto, was still mostly white before World War I (Edwards, 1968, p. 145). The mass influx of chicanos and Puerto Ricans has been largely a phenomenon of World War II and after.

The city has not of course brought automatic socioeconomic advancement, and certainly not instant advancement to ethnic minorities. The literature on minorities in the city has long painted a grim, if not desperate, picture of their lives there. In the nineteenth century, it was first the Irish and then the Jews, Italians, and other southern and eastern

*The Urban Institute, and professor of economics, University of California at Los Angeles (on leave). The author wishes to state that the views expressed are entirely his own. Some passages in this chapter are from Sowell, 1975 (in process). Complete publishing information can be found in the references at the end of the chapter.

111

Europeans whose lives were depicted in despairing terms, along with occasional references to the "squalor" and "depravity" of the Chinese immigrants.

These groups, now largely in the mainstream of American life by all the usual socioeconomic indicators, lived under physical conditions at least as squalid as those in the slums today. When the lower east side of New York City was a Jewish slum, it contained three times as many people per square mile as it has today (Kristol, 1966). When Manhattan's west side was an Irish slum, its rate of broken homes was 50 percent (Banfield, 1970, p. 72) — higher than that of black families today (Moynihan, 1965, p. 761). Mass violence by and against minorities then exceeded anything seen in the United States within the past generation; all the ghetto riots of the 1960s did not kill as many people as were killed in one riot in 1863 (Furnas, 1969, p. 702; National Advisory Commission of Civil Disorders, 1968, p. 115). The very concept of a "race riot" has been watered down to mean civil disorders within a racially segregated area, whereas in the nineteenth century it meant a massive clash between different racial, religious, or nationality groups.

While the urban problems of today are not unique, either in kind or in severity, the question is: Can we assume that they will be resolved for today's disadvantaged groups as they have been for their predecessors? Today's minorities are from a different cultural background, and in some cases carry biologically indelible color differences. The world itself is different — in mass media, in political climate, and in economic institutions. Even if today's urban minority problems are soluble, can they be solved by the methods or spontaneous patterns which historically marked the progress of earlier minorities? The sociological, economic, and political aspects of these questions will be considered in order.

SOCIOLOGICAL FACTORS

The negative effects of slums on those who live in them have long been a staple of sociological (and journalistic) thought, despite the problem of distinguishing correlation from causation. For many metropolitan areas, the slum problem has long been an ethnic minority problem. When Riis wrote his classic *How the Other Half Lives*, he found virtually no native-born Americans in the slums of New York (1970, p. 18). Similar patterns existed in other big cities. Occupationally as well, native-born, old stock Americans had left the bottom rungs of the ladder to the recent immigrants and the blacks (Jones, 1970, pp. 225, 312).

If the physical deterioration found in slums is merely correlated with such social pathology as crime, poverty, and family disorganization — without being a *cause* of it — then slums may be simply transit points for those passing through on their way to a better life elsewhere. If the negative human influences are the crucial problem of the slums, then slums may be a trap rather than a transit area — whether the human influences are primarily the life-styles of slum dwellers themselves or the institutions and practices of the larger society.

The older reform or muckraking literature had little doubt that the physical conditions of the slums *caused* many of the social ills found there. The relief of overcrowding and the provision of better sanitation and other public services were depicted not merely as "consumer" benefits to slum dwellers but as "investments" with a large and immediate payoff to society in the form of more productive and less destructive people in the lower classes. Much of the history of public housing in the United States since World War II has undermined, or even destroyed, that position. The government's demolition of the mammoth Pruitt–Igo housing project (von Eckhardt, 1972, p. B1) was a landmark in American social thought. "Slum clearance" will never hold the place it once held as a solution to social problems.

Housing exhibits a clear pattern of ecological succession. The housing which belonged to one ethnic group and income class in one period regularly passes on to another ethnic group or lower income class in another period. Viewed another way, it has been a common pattern for a minority arriving in a city to establish an initial neighborhood site from which it spreads out to other parts of the city. New arrivals to the city of the same ethnic group tend to settle at the initial site. Poverty conditions at the initial neighborhood site may therefore remain virtually unchanged for decades, while those families who began at the site spread successively farther out geographically and farther up in terms of socio-economic mobility. This spread may be into contiguous areas, where conditions permit, or there may be a leapfrogging of occupied and entrenched neighborhoods to establish new ethnic enclaves for the upwardly mobile.

One social consequence is that everyone may be painfully aware of the decline of his or her old neighborhood, while simultaneously everyone may be better housed than ever before. One research consequence is that a study of existing neighborhood residents distorts the experience of the group. One cannot tell the history even of slum dwellers by studying the lives of those who *remain* slum dwellers — implicitly ignoring the lives of their contemporaries who also *began* as slum dwellers. Elementary as this consideration is, it is repeatedly overlooked or ignored in empirical studies and generalizations about "grassroots" people. Although the housing patterns of blacks have long been different from the housing patterns of white ethnic groups, they are somewhat similar in showing clear intra- and intergroup ecological succession patterns.

All geographic mobility among disadvantaged minorities is not social mobility. Much is merely a rapid turnover of residences, long a characteristic of urban poverty groups in the United States. There are many consequences of this. For example, in some slum schools there is almost a 100 percent turnover of children from one school year to the next (Glazer and Moynihan, 1963, p. 127). Many credit-rating schemes used by department stores, banks, and other credit-granting institutions penalize the frequent mover — based on experience from the general population, which may or may not be applicable to subgroups where this is a common pattern among good credit risks as well as bad. Many sociopolitical schemes for "community involvement" implicitly assume that there *is* a community, rather than a geographical crossroads for transients. Such "community" schemes may in fact mean the unchallenged dominance by a handful of resident activists with no permanent constituency to whom they are accountable.

The ecological succession patterns have still another social implication: Intragroup segregation has long been a strong pattern among both black and white ethnic groups, though it has attracted far less attention than intergroup — and particularly racial — segregation. One of the problems of the black middle class has been that interracial segregation has in the past thwarted its efforts at intragroup segregation, despite repeated and sometimes desperate efforts to separate itself from lower socioeconomic strata. The question here is not whether this would have been philosophically, socially, or otherwise desirable from some "objective" point of view; the point is that internal segregation has obviously been highly *desired* by subgroups of blacks and whites. Indeed many academics who espouse all sorts of mixing of ethnic, economic, and social groups would not themselves associate with professors of education at their own universities. Racial segregation is more visible, and in some ways more vicious, than other forms of segregation, but it is by no means clear that it is more prevalent — or that it can discredit all forms of differentiation and separation.

One of the forms of differentiation which needs to be considered is that between the violence prone and the victims of violence. This is true not only for adults but perhaps particularly so regarding violence in school that is directed against "achieving" or "conforming" students. This form of ethnic self-destruction has attracted relatively little attention — perhaps because it does not lend itself to moralistic formulations or political interpretations — but it has long been a characteristic of low-income ethnic groups.

Among the influences on minorities in the city, besides the physical surroundings and the community (or lack of community), is the family. The family is important not only in terms of its size and stability but also in terms of its effectiveness in transmitting values and of the nature of the values it transmits.

Much has been made of the high incidence of broken homes among black families today, and this has been asserted to be a legacy of slavery's destructive impact on family life. What is remarkable about this assertion is how long it has remained unchallenged or untested. It might readily be tested in any of a number of ways — for example (1) by comparing the incidence of broken homes among blacks today with the incidence of broken homes among other low-socioeconomic groups (past and present) who were not enslaved, or (2) by comparing the incidence of broken homes in the ghetto today with the incidence of broken homes there in the past, nearer (or during) the era of slavery. The current incidence of broken homes among chicanos or Puerto Ricans is very similar to that among blacks today, and the incidence of broken homes in the low-income Irish west side of Manhattan at the time of World War I was somewhat higher than that in black ghettos today (Banfield, 1970, p. 72).

The incidence of broken homes in black ghettos in the past was lower than it is today. In Philadelphia in 1850, blacks born in slavery had a lower incidence of broken homes than blacks born free (Hershbert, 1971–72, p. 194; Pleck, 1972, pp. 18–25). The broken home, and even the matrifocal intact home, has been characteristic of lower socioeconomic groups generally, whether black or white (Rainwater, 1966, p. 190; Gans, 1965, pp. 238–39). Statistics show the unemployment rate among black males to be highly correlative with the divorce rates a few months later (Moynihan, 1965, p. 768). It is apparently economics, more so than history, which contributes to the high incidence of broken homes.

Family size patterns are likewise not easy to characterize. The old adage that "the rich get rich and the poor have children" still has a measure of truth in it, but a more complex pattern emerges when we compare disadvantaged ethnic minorities with the general population. In the lower income bracket black families have more children than white families at the same income level, while in the upper income brackets, black families are *smaller* than white families (Moynihan, 1965, p. 759). Black families headed by professional or technically trained men do not have enough children to reproduce themselves. The great maldistribution of children by income class is further aggravated by the fact that income distribution is slightly more *unequal* among blacks than among whites (U.S. Department of Commerce, various years). That is, the top 10 percent of blacks earn a higher proportion of the total income of the black population than the top 10 percent of whites earn of the total income of the white population. There are several important social consequences of this situation:

(1) The painful struggle from poverty to middle-class income, which a certain proportion of American blacks make in each generation, has to be largely done all over again in the next generation because middle-class blacks have so few children to inherit their advantages.

(2) The bulk of black children come from those classes with the least income to support them, and the least education or successful experience to impart.

(3) The enormous economic disparities within the black population — between the only child of a doctor or engineer and the large family of a laborer or welfare mother — create great emotional strains (envy, suspicion, guilt, and so forth) within the black community, inhibiting cooperative efforts to advance the race as a whole.

The reasons for the extremely small size of black middle-class families — ranging from 0.7 to 1.6 children in various studies (Frazier, 1969, pp. 330–31) — are undoubtedly many, but it would be difficult to assess their relative importance. One factor is that blacks of the same middle-class *income* level as whites have less *wealth* (Brimmer and Terrell, 1971, p. 21) and so are less able to afford children. They would tend to have less wealth because they are more likely to be newly middle class, to be from families too poor to have left them even modest estates, and to have relatives who would be less able to help them and more likely to require their help in an emergency. The newly achieved middle-class income position is probably of more value to blacks as well, both because it is new and hard won, and because it removes them from the worst forms of racism.

Finally, middle-class blacks are likely to come from lower class homes with excessive numbers of children and to react strongly against their own childhood experiences. Perhaps as generations pass and the middle-class blacks become familiar with and more confident in their new status, some of the reasons for severely restricting their family size will erode and more normal distribution of children will evolve in the black population.

There has been a common phenomenon in most races and nationalities, at most periods of history, that the poor have more children than the rich. Among low-income blacks, families have been even larger than among most other low-income Americans. This is clearly not a racial characteristic, as shown by the opposite pattern among middle-class blacks and by the unusually small families of most urban blacks before the twentieth century. Whatever the reason, its consequences are very serious and reach beyond the individual family to affect the economic and social progress of American blacks as a whole. For example, much publicity has been given to the fact that a high percentage of black males failed the U.S. Army mental test, and this has even been used to support a theory of racial inferiority. However, *three-quarters* of all black males who failed the mental test came from families with four or more children. Half of them came from families of six or more children (Moynihan, 1965, p. 759). Among either blacks or whites, mental development tends to be greatest among small families. The Jews' long tradition of small families is undoubtedly a factor in their intellectual achievements. Many studies of high IQ children, prominent men and women, and other "success" groups, have found a great overrepresentation of the "only child" or the first born, who is necessarily an only child for at least a time. Conversely, twins — who share divided attention from the moment they enter the world — average lower IQs than single-birth children. In short, family size has implications well beyond the family itself. The direct financial cost of supporting a large family, serious as it is, may be less important than the racial and social consequences of sending forth large numbers of people with less preparation than that required to cope with the complexities and frustrations of modern life.

Since family size varies by income and education, a considerable part of the ethnic variation in number of children is in reality a variation in income and education among ethnic groups. The fact that blacks of high income and advanced education have fewer children than whites in similar categories, even though blacks in general have more children than whites in general, is only one example of this. Puerto Ricans have more children born per woman than blacks or than almost any other ethnic group. Yet Puerto Ricans who have finished high school have fewer children per woman than any of these ethnic groups — and fewer than the national average for high school graduates (U.S. Department of Commerce, various years). Puerto Ricans also have the highest incidence of sterility operations of any social group in the United States (Glazer and Moynihan, 1963, pp. 98–99). Chicanos have the largest number of children per woman in childbearing years of any major ethnic group, but do not have as many per woman as *any* of the other minorities, when we compare high school graduates only (U.S. Department of Commerce, various years).

Economic Factors

The pattern of ecological succession found in ethnic housing applies equally to ethnic occupational patterns. In some cases this has meant that later arriving groups replace earlier groups in occupations which the latter abandoned for better ones — as the Italians replaced the Jews as coal and ice peddlers and replaced the Irish as miners, dock workers, and railroad workers (Foerster, 1970, pp. 339, 350, 356, 358). Sometimes, however, the later arriving groups simply displaced the earlier groups by working for lower wages, performing the work better, or simply being more acceptable to racial prejudices. Northern urban blacks who had achieved some foothold in a variety of lower middle-class occupations by mid-nineteenth century were widely displaced from these occupations by the arrival of masses of European immigrants over the next several decades (Hershbert, 1971–72, p. 191; Litwack, 1970, pp. 165–66). The Chinese and Japanese immigrants on the West Coast displaced many others in low-socioeconomic occupations, arousing the special hostility of the Irish, who were overrepresented in such work (Hosokawa, 1969, p. 67; Wittke, 1970, pp. 191–92).

In labor unions as well, the pattern of ecological succession was apparent in cases where a particular immigrant group was regarded by the unions first as "scabs," were then accepted as members, and ultimately accounted for most of the membership, while the officialdom continued to be drawn from other ethnic groups that had earlier been the predominant element in the membership. The Italian immigrants, for example, were first rejected by unions, were widely used by employers as strike breakers, but ultimately came to form a major part of unions in which the Irish often formed the leadership. An analogous leadership-membership situation has existed in the International Ladies Garment Workers Unions, where a large black and Puerto Rican membership has been led by Jewish officials.

American blacks were in some cases first driven out of occupations which they had dominated for years by the rising labor unions (railroads and the construction industry being prime examples), and were then prevented from entering these "white men's jobs" by devices ranging from direct "white only" union membership rules to exacting mental tests from which existing practitioners were exempted by grandfather clauses and other special dispensations. Although blacks were the most severely discriminated against by labor unions, as well as by other institutions, discrimination also hit minorities in general. American labor unions were for many years in the forefront of opposition to continued open immigration, and were politically instrumental in achieving the eventual exclusions in the immigration laws which in the 1920s put a stop to the greatest mass migration in history.

Labor unions have been in a philosophically ambiguous position vis-à-vis minorities. The general philosophy of unionism emphasizes solidarity and democratic values, while the economics of their situation forces the unions to protect the gains of their own current membership, even if it is done at the expense (exclusion) of other working-class people, and the politics of union office holding also requires a healthy respect for the prejudices of the voting members. Unions have therefore supported many racially "liberal" public policies while at the same time retaining racial and ethnic restrictions, exclusions, and preferences in their internal affairs.

The deliberate and explicit policy positions of labor unions regarding racial and ethnic minorities may not be the most important of their effects, however. The unions are one aspect of a more general economic phenomenon — the institutional structuring, "rationalization," or "bureaucratization" of labor markets. The effect of this is not peculiar to ethnic minorities, but the differences between the relatively unstructured labor markets of the nineteenth century and the relatively controlled labor markets of today may affect the differing opportunities available to European immigrants in the nineteenth century and analogous disadvantaged minorities today.

It is not necessary to imagine anything so extreme as the economists' theoretical model of "perfect competition" as a contrast to what may be called the "bureaucratic" labor market. The latter will include not only unionized labor markets but any markets where employment and earnings reflect structured organizational policies rather than the direct effects of supply and demand. Thus bureaucratic labor markets include civil service systems, labor markets in "cost-plus" industries (government contractors, public utilities), low-wage markets directly affected by minimum wage laws, and corporations with policies of hiring from the bottom and promoting from within. It is obvious that labor unions and minimum wage laws raise the earnings rate above what it would be in the absence of these. The normal tendency of wages set above the level they would otherwise reach is to increase the number of persons seeking employment and reduce the number it is profitable for the employer to hire — i.e., to create a surplus of labor. Surplus labor in turn implies that the employer can more cheaply indulge any racial or ethnic prejudices he may have, since there is an excess of applicants anyway. The same is true under "cost-plus" pricing. Here the employer is not *forced* (by unions or laws) to offer higher wages than the market would require, but it costs him nothing to do so, and thus he may freely raise wages to a level that will create a surplus of qualified applicants from which he can choose only those who meet his racial, ethnic, sex, or personality prejudices (Alchian and Kessel, 1962, pp. 157–75; Sowell, 1973, pp. 1–25). Obviously the losers here, too, are likely to be members of minority groups.

Civil service systems, though often called "merit" systems, have long been subject in practice to many influences other than individual merit. Political pressures virtually ensure that low-level civil service jobs will be paid more than the market rate for similar qualifications, just as the same pressures cause high-level civil service jobs to be insufficiently paid to attract the quantity and the quality of applicants needed. There is, in short, a labor surplus at the bottom of the civil service job ladder, creating the preconditions for discrimination among excessive applicants. Political counterpressure (primarily from the minority itself) may offset this during some periods, but not during others (Sowell, 1973, pp. 9–11). Moreover, the civil service tests required for employment in low-level jobs often have little relationship to the actual work itself, but they test educational achievement levels in a way detrimental to disadvantaged groups (The Urban Institute, 1971). Nineteenth century minorities faced no such hurdles in getting low-level jobs.

The policy of hiring at the bottom and promoting from within is a little more complicated but leads to similar results. Where such a company policy prevails, the low-level "entrance" jobs become steps on an occupational ladder. Therefore applicants for these jobs may be evaluated not merely in terms of whether they can perform the particular work directly involved in the job, but also in terms of the prospects for their promotion. In short, applicants must be overqualified for the low-level jobs. Many people who are capable of doing the work required may therefore be "unemployable" under these institutional arrangements. For those who meet these artificially high requirements, there will be more pay than in a less controlled market, but those who do not meet the requirements may become "unemployable."

It should be noted that "unemployability" is a function of price: Everyone is unemployable at some rate of pay. Raising the rate of pay disproportionately excludes those most recently arrived and least skilled or experienced in the urban labor market: minorities compared to the general population, and within minorities, the new teenage and young adult workers in particular. Numbers of studies have shown a pronounced impact of minimum wages on the unemployment rate of black teenagers (Kosters and Welch, 1972, p. 330; Brozen, 1962, pp. 103–09). Unemployment rates of 30 percent have been common among blacks in the sixteen to nineteen age bracket, and in urban areas, even higher rates have been common. In contrast, among black males in the 25 to 44 age bracket, the unemployment rate has exceeded 8 percent in only one of the past ten years, and has never exceeded 10 percent for any of those years.

It is not only the level of pay but the *system* of payment which has created employment problems for contemporary minorities which nineteenth century immigrants did not have to face. Payment by piece rate was much more common in earlier times. This facilitated the employment of persons across a wide spectrum of job capabilities. The immigrant just off the boat, with no industrial or commercial skills, was almost equally as employable as an experienced native worker. Women and children were also employable for the same reason, even in jobs geared to adult males. Each person could be paid in proportion to whatever he or she actually produced. Increasingly, however, payment is by time, whether by hours or by the week; and the minimum blocks of time tend also to be greater as public mores, union rules, civil service regulations, and laws on hiring and firing limit an employer's ability to halt the employment of someone whose work is substandard. In short, work standards themselves are artificially raised, and the difficulties of eliminating *ex post* those who do not meet these standards increase the employers' incentives to hire those known *ex ante* to be at a higher level of qualification than absolutely necessary for the work itself.

Since jobs are a source not only of current income but also of work experience with a future value, the losses suffered through unemployment cannot be estimated by the immediate pay loss alone. This is particularly true for those urban ethnic minorities that are in a process of transition from one way of life to another. The nineteenth century immigrant minorities were not faced with a double-or-nothing situation in which only the best qualified could find steady work — and that at artificially high rates of pay. They could *all* find a place somewhere on the occupational ladder. Most had a higher labor force participation rate than the general population. So, too, did blacks — in every census from 1890 to 1940. Now the black labor force participation rate is below that of the white population, and the gap is widening. A further complication is that compulsory education laws keep young people from gaining experience as a result of raising the age at which they can leave school and work full time. Theoretically, the additional schooling could offset the reduced work experience, but increasingly both the economic and the social value of that additional schooling has been questioned, and it has even been suggested that that value may be negative (Banfield, 1970, pp. 148–57).

There is not only a general contrast between the constraints faced by poor and low-skill minorities as they entered the urban labor markets in the nineteenth and twentieth centuries, but constraints facing today's disadvantaged minorities in many cases were created by the former disadvantaged minorities now consolidating their improved positions. This is obvious in the case of many labor union exclusions, but it is no less true in the case of civil service exams, minimum wage laws, and laws keeping young people in school and out of the labor market. It is also blatantly obvious in the severely restrictive immigration laws of the 1920s which organized labor had advocated for years. These laws, however, produce no identifiable American victims.

Civil service exams protect those ethnic groups who have already achieved an educational level sufficient to pass them. It protects them from the ethnic prejudices which they encountered from nativist employers in both municipal and federal civil service in times past, and which could conceivably become important barriers to them today in the administration of such a system. It more immediately also protects them from the competition of other minorities that have not yet achieved their educational levels — particularly if these levels are measured by results rather than by years in school. To some extent this is the inevitable result of work capability differentials due to different historical circumstances. But for many routine (often manual) jobs, pencil and paper tests have little or no bearing on work performance. It is little more than a domestic tariff barrier to protect the "haves" from the "have nots."

Minimum wage laws are another advantage for those already advantaged. This is so not only for direct competitors for a given job, but also where the employer substitutes one job level for another in the production process. Most things can be produced with any of a large number of possible combinations of skilled and unskilled labor. A law that raises the price of unskilled labor biases the choice of production methods toward a more skilled mixture. The work is effectively transferred from one group to another, even if the workers involved are so dissimilar they are not popularly thought of as competitors. This is often an ethnic transfer as well, where the lowest level workers are from today's disadvantaged groups and the higher level workers from yesterday's disadvantaged groups. This is particularly likely to be true in large metropolitan areas, where both groups of minorities are concentrated.

The economic effect of laws raising the age of school attendance or labor force participation depends upon the relative value of the schooling and the work experience. As with most economic issues, it is not a question whether A is more valuable than B in any absolute sense, but whether incremental changes in A produce more or less a given result than incremental changes in B, *given* a certain amount of each. The theoretical problem of determining the rate of return from education is an almost bottomless pit of complexities. However, a definitive theoretical solution is not a prerequisite for practical judgments and actions. The fact that physicists are still studying the nature of electricity does not prevent us from having light bulbs, refrigerators, or television sets.

The practical judgments in education vary so much by individual ability and inclinations that individual decisions may be preferable in any case. A common denominator between nineteenth and twentieth century urban minorities has been their resistance to compulsory attendance laws. These laws were evaded not only by less education-conscious groups, such as Italian immigrants, but even by such a classic education-oriented group as the Jews (Cordasco, 1968, p. 182). Violations of child labor laws among the lower east side Jews were among the "scandals" uncovered by Riis (1970, p. 82) in the 1890s. This was done not frivolously, blindly, or self-destructively, but because these families judged for themselves that further education beyond some point was no longer in their economic self-interest. Riis (p. 71) noted the high work capacity and strong savings propensities among these Jewish families in the 1890s — thus they clearly were not oblivious to the future. Their judgments happened to differ from those of Riis and the school authorities, and it is by no means clear that east side Jews were wrong.

Today's disadvantaged minorities face the same kinds of laws, but now they are more stringently enforced and extend over a longer span of a child's life. Indeed these laws today cover a period of life in which the term "child" is questionable and when the capacity for physical destruction has vastly increased. The attitude of alienation and habits of undisciplined rebellion must be counted among the negative effects of extended compulsory schooling on today's disadvantaged minorities. There are obvious advantages to established workers in having millions of potential competitors held off the labor market in what has been aptly termed "aging vats" rather than educational institutions.

POLITICAL FACTORS

Ethnic politics has long been a colorful feature of American life, and some of the most striking American political leaders have come from its ethnic minorities. The economic rise of some groups has proceeded in step with their political rise, and while everyone knows that correlation is not causation, there has nevertheless been a general tendency to consider political muscle a major factor — even a precondition — for minority economic advance. One major study of ethnic political life (Levy and Kramer, 1972, p. 24) has argued that ethnic groups in general must follow the pattern established by blacks, even though (1) most of the other ethnic groups already have higher incomes and other socioeconomic indicators than blacks, and (2) blacks are doing best in the North, where their political participation has declined (p. 18).

The economic effect of political power (however measured) is seldom studied empirically, though assertions abound. A real study would be a major undertaking, but even casual empiricism turns up many counterexamples to the prevailing assumptions — and these counterexamples do not become "exceptions" merely because the prevailing assumptions have been unchallenged for so long. Two of the most successful minorities in the United States today, in terms of incomes, occupations, or education, have had virtually zero political power throughout their history in the United States — the Chinese and the Japanese. The most successful American minority in politics has been the Irish — who were already in control of major American cities by the middle of the nineteenth century but were still overwhelmingly working in unskilled jobs more than a generation later. Italian-Americans, who were very late arriving on the political scene and have yet to achieve the political success of the Irish, have nevertheless had slightly higher average incomes than the Irish, who were dominant in politics generations earlier. Chicanos have had nothing approaching the same political participation — as either voters or officeholders — as blacks, but nevertheless have slightly higher incomes.

The same empirical argument can be made historically as is made cross-sectionally. The high point of black political power was during the Reconstruction period in the South — and it was precisely during this period that black employment in skilled occupations suffered a massive retrogression from which it has never recovered. Blacks in the northern cities made substantial economic and social advances in the last two decades of the nineteenth century with virtually no political power, achieving rates of business ownership and residential integration never again reached after the mass influx of southern black migrants brought increased political power and reduced socioeconomic status. There is no need to prove too much — counterexamples could also be marshaled: the rise of black incomes and occupations (relatively, as well as absolutely) in the wake of the civil rights movement of the 1960s, the increase in minority employment in government (local and national) wherever minorities have acquired political muscle, and the disastrous economic losses suffered by the Japanese-Americans because of the political climate during World War II when they were interned.

The point here is not to show political power to be either impotent or omnipotent, or even to strike a judicious balance. The point is to show it to be an open question — with many historical trends suggesting an almost random relationship between the two. Some would argue that if political power has *any* effect at any time, that is reason enough to seek it. However, this overlooks the fact that political power seeking has a cost — not only in dollars but in foregone options and orientations which might have a higher payoff. The leaders of the Chinese-American community deliberately chose to stay out of politics and had sufficient power to quash individual Chinese who had other ideas (Light, 1972, p. 174). Clearly the Chinese leaders considered the cost of politics too high, and it is not obvious that they were wrong. The average Chinese in America today has a higher income and a higher occupational status than the average white American.

Rather than attempt a resolution of the question of the positive vs the negative aspects of political routes to ethnic advancement, let us instead concentrate on the limitations and counterproductive aspects of political action — on the assumption that there is already ample material available on the benefits of political activism. One of the problems of politics is that the politician's vision is short run — seldom extending beyond the next election. Within that time frame he may be a genius at knowing what the voters want *right now* — even if they will want something different in five years, and even if what they want will bring disaster a generation hence. It was only a decade ago that any opposition to integration was political suicide in a black neighborhood — even in neighborhoods that now want no part of "whitey."

A decade ago it was the hallmark of forward-looking liberalism on the national scene to be for all-out efforts for accelerated economic growth rates ("to get America moving again"), and either opposition or just plain doubts were the hallmarks of moribund conservatism. Today these roles are reversed. The point here is not to pass judgment on the substantive merits of these policies but to indicate the wide swings of political opinion, which will allow few policies to be pursued with any consistency for any long period of time. Ethnic problems and racial problems seem the least likely to yield to short-run "instant solutions," and long-run solutions are not the politician's strong point.

Most ethnic groups — if not *all* American ethnic groups — have undergone great transformations over the years, so that the "rise" of the Irish or the Jews (and others) has not been a simple acceptance of given groups by the larger society but rather mutual accommodation — not only among peoples but between groups from a nonindustrial background — to the unyielding requirements of technology and urban living. Politicians are not only ill equipped to aid in this transformation, they are in many ways counterproductive. Politicians may promote schemes which confer immediate tangible benefits on their constituents, but they are in no position to demand adjustments by their constituents to economic or technological realities. Indeed the logic of their political situation demands that they emphasize the importance of the benefits they are in a position to confer and minimize or deny the adjustments the constituents must make in their attitudes and life-styles. Politically devised programs can teach job skills but cannot as easily demand work discipline — regardless of which is more urgently needed. They can build new schools for constituents but not demand that the constituents send their children to these schools with a better attitude and more discipline, regardless of which is more urgently needed. Indeed the politician must often *misrepresent* which is more urgently needed.

Finally, politics by nature is an elite field — however much the leaders may speak in the name of "the people." Sometimes this has been blatantly obvious, as in times when Irish politicians represented Italian constituents or when white politicians represented black districts. It is no less true when physical similarities permit social camouflage. The poor and the disadvantaged, almost by definition, do not have the money or the organizational experience to run political campaigns. This is painfully apparent when rich politicians represent poor constituents and vote for measures obviously contrary to the constituents' interest. It is no less true when "sincere" reformers try to help the poor. These reformers *observe* the poor but do not *experience* what the poor experience. The history of American political reform is a history of almost unbroken opposition to the reformers by ethnic minorities (Handlin, 1951, pp. 218–21; 1970, pp. 200, 206; Shannon, 1969, p. 80). The great political machines attacked by the reformers were almost invariably supported by ethnic minorities. The compulsory education laws promoted by the reformers were opposed and evaded by the ethnic groups. The honest and impersonal bureaucracies built by the reformers destroyed the crooked but accessible ward heelers who got *results* for people too uneducated, unorganized, and uninfluential to budge massive "good government."

SUMMARY

The big question in discussions of disadvantaged minorities in the city is: Can their problems be solved? Despite much that can be done and must be done, the ultimate answer to this particular question may be "no." This does not mean that the problem is invincible or that progress will stop. The city — and especially the central city — has long been the focus of particular kinds of social problems. As successive groups have evolved some resolution of their problems, they have typically moved away from the central city, and often outside the city entirely. If the focus is *people*, and not municipal boundaries, the future looks more promising. Yet political pressures tend to force cities, as such, into the center of attention. Politicians are elected from particular districts, and what happens within the imaginary lines which bound their domain is extremely important. But that is no reason for anyone else to take at face value their cries to "save the city." Humanitarian feelings toward one's fellow man do not imply an obligation to perpetuate a particular kind of political subdivision or a particular form of residential organization. There are many within those subdivisions who are not poor or disadvantaged, and who are in fact quite adroit at intercepting money intended to help those who are. Urban renewal may be enough to arouse memories (and turn stomachs).

To "solve the problems of the city" implies not only that it is the city (rather than the people) which is our central concern, but also that there is some process to be engaged in by persons qualified to "solve" social problems. It would be hard to construct an impressive list of social problems which have been solved in this manner, and all too easy to recall numerous problems which have been made worse by grand designs. In a sense, this is a vindication of the democratic creed — for it suggests an unsuspected reservoir of abilities, determination, and resourcefulness even among those in whom those attributes are so casually assumed to be absent.

REFERENCES

Alchian, Armen A.; and Kessel, Reuben A. "Competition, Monopoly, and the Pursuit of Money." In *Aspects of Labor Economics*, National Bureau of Economic Research. Princeton, New Jersey: Princeton University Press. 1962.

Banfield, Edward C. *The Unheavenly City*. Boston: Little, Brown and Co. 1970.

Brimmer, Andrew F.; and Terrell, Henry S. "The Economic Potential of Black Capitalism." *The Black Politician* (April 1971).

Brozen, Yale. "The Effects of Statutory Minimum Wage Increases on Teenage Unemployment." *Journal of Law and Economics* (October 1962).

Cordasco, Francesco. Editor. *Jacob Riis Revisited.* New York: Anchor Books. 1968.

Edwards, G. Franklin. Editor. *E. Franklin Frazier on Race Relations.* Chicago: University of Chicago Press. 1968.

Foerster, Robert F. *The Italian Immigration of Our Times.* New York: Arno Press. 1970.

Frazier, E. Franklin. *The Negro Family in the United States.* Chicago: University of Chicago Press. 1969.

Furnas, J. C. *The Americans.* New York: G. P. Putnam & Sons. 1969.

Gans, Herbert F. *The Urban Villagers.* New York: The Free Press. 1965.

Glazer, Nathan; and Moynihan, Daniel Patrick. *Beyond the Melting Pot.* Cambridge, Massachusetts: M.I.T. Press. 1963.

Handlin, Oscar. *Boston's Immigrants.* New York: Atheneum. 1970.

————. *The Uprooted.* New York: Grosset & Dunlap, Inc. 1951.

Hershbert, Theodore. "Free Blacks in Antebellum Philadelphia: A Study of Ex-Slaves, Freeborn, and Socioeconomic Decline." *Journal of Social History* (Winter 1971–72).

Hosokawa, Bill. *Nisei: The Quiet Americans.* New York: William Morrow and Co., Inc. 1969.

Jones, Maldwyn Allen. *American Immigration.* Chicago: University of Chicago Press. 1970.

Kosters, Marvin; and Welch, Finis. "The Effects of Minimum Wages on the Distribution of Changes in Aggregate Employment." *American Economic Review* (June 1972).

Kristol, Irving. "The Negro Today Is Like the Immigrant Yesterday." New York *Times.* (September 11, 1966).

Levy, Mark R.; and Kramer, Michael S. *The Ethnic Factor.* New York: Simon & Schuster, Inc. 1972.

Light, Ivan H. *Ethnic Enterprise in America.* Berkeley: University of California Press. 1972.

Moynihan, Daniel Patrick. "Employment, Income, and the Negro Family." *Daedalus* (Fall 1965).

National Advisory Commission on Civil Disorders. *Report of the National Advisory Commission on Civil Disorders.* New York: E. P. Dutton. 1968.

Litwack, Leon F. *North of Slavery.* Chicago: University of Chicago Press. 1970.

Pleck, Elizabeth H. "The Two-Parent Household: Black Family Structure in Late Nineteenth Century Boston." *Journal of Social History* (Fall 1972).

Rainwater, Lee. "Crucible of Identity: The Negro Lower-Class Family." *Daedalus* (Winter 1966).

Riis, Jacob A. *How the Other Half Lives.* Cambridge, Massachusetts: Harvard University Press. 1970.

Shannon, William V. *The American Irish.* New York: The Macmillan Company. 1969.

Sowell, Thomas. *Race and Economics.* New York: David McKay Company, Inc. 1975.

—————. "Race and the Market." *Review of Black Political Economy* (Summer 1973).

Urban Institute, The. *The Validity and Discriminatory Impact of the Federal Service Entrance Examination.* Washington, D.C.: The Urban Institute. 1971.

U.S. Department of Commerce, Bureau of the Census. *Census of Population.* Series P-20. Washington, D.C.: U.S. Government Printing Office. Various years.

von Eckhardt, Wolf. "Death of the 'City of the Future.' " *Washington Post.* June 24, 1972.

Wittke, Carl. *The Irish in America.* New York: Russell & Russell. 1970.

7
Low -Wage Workers in Metropolitan Labor Markets

ALBERT REES*

This chapter concentrates on the problems of the low-wage worker in metropolitan labor markets. Low-wage workers are of special interest for several reasons: First, they are one of the largest components of the poor in central cities and in the older, less residential suburbs. Second, they figure prominently in the newest theoretical approach to urban labor markets, the so-called dual or segmented labor market theory. Third, they are the supposed beneficiaries of the minimum wage law and of many manpower training programs, but they are excluded from most existing income maintenance programs, such as Aid to Families with Dependent Children. In short, one of the main policy concerns about metropolitan labor markets has been how best to help the low-wage urban worker. Unfortunately many of these policy concerns have not been much illuminated by labor market research. In the remarks that follow, I shall touch on several disparate aspects of this general question.

DUAL LABOR MARKET THEORY AND UPWARD MOBILITY

The dual labor market hypothesis has been succinctly stated by Piore (1972, p. 2). According to him:

> The basic hypothesis of the dual labor market was that the labor market is divided into two essentially distinct sectors,

* Professor of economics and faculty associate, Industrial Relations Section, Princeton University.

131

termed the *primary* and the *secondary* sectors. The former offers jobs with relatively high wages, good working conditions, chances of advancement, equity and due process in the administration of work rules and, above all, employment stability. Jobs in the secondary sector, by contrast, tend to be low paying, with poorer working conditions, little chance of advancement; a highly personalized relationship between workers and supervisors which leaves wide latitude for favoritism and is conducive to harsh and capricious work discipline; and with considerable instability in jobs and a high turnover among the labor force. The hypothesis was designed to explain the problems of disadvantaged, particularly black workers in urban areas, which had previously been diagnosed as one of unemployment.

The jobs in the secondary market as described by Piore well characterize those held by the workers I shall refer to here as "the working poor."

There are, however, some important problems with the dual and segmented labor market theory that should be noted at this point. In the first place, dual labor market theory is not really a theory, but rather a taxonomy. Taxonomy can be an important tool of science; indeed in biology it has been an indispensable tool. However, while evidence can refute or fail to refute a hypothesis, it cannot refute a taxonomy. Taxonomies must be judged not on whether they are false, but on whether they are useful. They are most useful when different observers can easily agree on which cases are to be classified in a given category, a criterion that is generally met by the familiar industry and occupational classifications. Unfortunately, the dual labor market hypothesis does not seem to meet this test.

The usefulness of the dual labor market taxonomy is greatly reduced because it characterizes two extremes of the job spectrum and attempts to force all of the intervening territory into boxes with labels that describe the extremes. In particular, the taxonomy suffers because of its insistence that opportunities for advancement are a necessary characteristic of a primary job. When a job is good enough, one doesn't care too much whether there are many opportunities for advancement. Consider the case of a journeyman plumber or pipefitter. Once he has completed his apprenticeship, he can advance only by becoming a foreman, a contractor, or a union officer, and these opportunities are severely limited. However, the wage of a journeyman plumber or pipefitter in many metropolitan areas is now $10.00 an hour or more, plus good fringe benefits, and despite occasional unemployment, annual earnings often exceed $16,000. Surely no one would argue on grounds of the lack of opportunity for advancement that this job is in the secondary labor market. A similar argument at a somewhat lower income level would apply to workers in automobile assembly plants, where there are few skilled jobs, but semiskilled workers have good earnings.

At the low-wage end of the job spectrum, the focus of the dual labor market literature on opportunities for advancement is much more relevant. Even here, this literature tends to exaggerate both the number of low-wage jobs that are also dead-end jobs and the number of dead-end jobs that are low wage. Counterexamples can be offered on both scores. The jobs of bagger and boxboy in a supermarket are low wage and usually part time, and require no training or experience, yet there is a clear line of progression to clerk, department manager, and store manager, though with sharply diminishing opportunities beyond the level of full-time clerk. Indeed supermarket chains are among the rare organizations, like police and fire departments, that have no separate system of training and recruitment for their officer corps — almost everyone comes up through the ranks. It is literally true that many of the top managers of food chains started as bag boys.

Conversely, the job of janitor requires little education or training, offers almost no opportunities for advancement, is considered menial, and is frequently filled by blacks and members of other minority groups. Surely, then, it is in the secondary labor market. Yet I have seen some collective bargaining agreements in northern metropolitan areas covering workers in food warehouses and food processing plants that specify janitors' wage rates in excess of $5.00 an hour. Since the work is steady, annual earnings may exceed $10,000. These janitors, at least, are not among the working poor. Moreover, where they are represented by a labor organization as powerful as the International Brotherhood of Teamsters, it is unlikely that they are subject to harsh and capricious work discipline. One could argue that high-wage janitors are in the primary sector and low-wage janitors are in the secondary sector, but then one violates the assumption that jobs in the two sectors are distinguished by skill. More generally, it throws away information to use a continuous variable like wages to create dichotomies or other sets of discrete categories because measures are a more powerful tool of science than classifications.

Having made the point that present versions of dual and segmented labor market theory are too simplistic, I do not mean to belabor it further. What is of interest here are the implications of this line of thought for further research. The chief implication I draw is that we need to know much more than we do about occupational mobility, especially upward mobility out of low-wage, menial jobs. Which are in fact the dead-end jobs? What are the characteristics of upwardly mobile workers? How much do training programs promote occupational mobility? How different are occupational mobility patterns for different ethnic groups?

Research into all of these questions has until recently been hampered by the absence of a major longitudinal data set that includes occupational data. The Social Security records, which are wonderful for studying geographical and industrial mobility, are of course completely devoid of occupational information. Fortunately, we now have the new data collected by Herbert Parnes and his associates at Ohio State which makes available new longitudinal information much richer in detail than Social Security records. I need not call for new research into occupational mobility — it is already under way.

MINIMUM WAGES AND YOUTH UNEMPLOYMENT

The minimum wage under the Fair Labor Standards Act for most covered industries was $1.60 an hour in 1973. In May 1974, the hourly minimum wage rose to $2.00. It will increase to $2.10 in January 1975, and will reach $2.30 in 1976. For purposes of wage stabilization, however, a low-wage worker was defined in the 1973 amendments to the Economic Stabilization Act as one who earns less than $3.50 an hour, a figure more than twice the 1973 minimum wage under the Fair Labor Standards Act. Public policy is thus mildly schizophrenic in defining low wages.

The view of professional economists is no more unified. On the one hand we have such radical economists as Bennett Harrison and Thomas Vietorisz calling for an immediate increase in the minimum wage to $3.00, so that the head of a household of four earning the minimum wage would be above a new poverty line, redefined to reflect better the high living costs of northern metropolitan areas. On the other hand we have a number of econometric studies that seem to show that the minimum wage is a major deterrent to youth employment, especially part-time employment by teenagers still in school (Welch, 1973).

One proposal that attempts to reconcile these divergent views is the proposal to raise the minimum wage for those aged twenty and over, but to have a lower minimum wage for teenagers. Amendments of this sort to the bills to raise the minimum wage were offered in Congress but were greeted with cries of outrage by the AFL-CIO. Such a system, the unions declared, would induce employers to discharge fathers in order to replace them with their sons. The labor movement, in arguing for higher minimum wages, generally argues that increases will have negligible employment effects. This implies an extremely low elasticity of substitution between capital and labor. However, in the case of the special youth minimum wage, they argue for an enormously high elasticity of substitution between experienced and inexperienced labor. I strongly suspect that they are wrong on both scores.

Early research showing strong employment effects of the minimum wage on youth was not entirely convincing; recent studies have been much more carefully done. Let me offer here one piece of casual empiricism that tends to support them. In Great Britain, where on the average youth leave school at a younger age than in the United States, there has been no problem of unemployed youth. Unemployment rates for teenagers are often below those of adults. Perhaps this is because of better vocational guidance in Great Britain. However, it is surely assisted by a wage structure that traditionally and uniformly pays teenagers less than their elders. If a job pays £21 a week to an adult, it will typically pay £15 a week to a fifteen-year-old school leaver, who will get an automatic increase of £1 a week on each birthday until he reaches the adult rate. Teenagers can be a bargain for a British employer, despite their inexperience and their high turnover. For an American employer, they tend to be employees of last resort.

Proposals which argue that one worker earning the minimum wage should be able to support a family of four at a level of decency assume that heads of one-earner families of four in fact receive the minimum wage. Perhaps this is still true in southern sawmills or work-clothing factories. It must be rare, however, in northern metropolitan areas. The impact of the minimum wage in these areas is basically on large covered firms in retailing and services, such as McDonald's and Woolworth's, and most of the affected employees are teenagers and married women who are secondary earners. For the household head earning the minimum wage, income maintenance programs such as the negative income tax offer alternative ways to alleviate poverty that seem likely to have substantially smaller adverse effects on employment. Moreover, the decrease in employment induced by income maintenance arises on the supply side of the market; i.e., it is voluntary rather than involuntary separation from employment.

However, the need to speculate on such matters suggests that we still know less about low-wage workers in metropolitan areas than we should. Much research on the minimum wage has focused on employment effects in low-wage industries such as southern pine lumber, work clothing, and hosiery. Such industries are generally located outside the major metropolitan areas. Other studies deal with the economy as a whole. Few if any deal explicitly with metropolitan areas.

In 1963, when data were gathered for the study of the Chicago labor market area directed by George P. Shultz and myself, we found one manufacturing firm in that high-wage area which never paid more than the federal minimum wage for most production jobs, and was nevertheless not short of labor. Are there still such firms? What would be the impact of the increase in the minimum to $2.10, $2.30, or even $3.00 on the employment of blacks and other minority groups, or on the employment of teenagers? Research that would answer such questions would not be hard to design, and would have great policy relevance.

INCOME MAINTENANCE PROGRAMS FOR THE WORKING POOR

The major existing income maintenance programs are all designed to provide income to those who are not at work. Very little — almost nothing — is done to provide supplementary income to the low-wage worker who has a full-time job and a large family and whose household lives in poverty. It is one of the tragic ironies of our system that many such families in northern cities could live better if the father deserted, making the family eligible for welfare. There is much resentment among the working poor against a welfare system that provides more money to families with no worker than the low-wage worker takes home after working hard all week.

In August 1969, President Nixon proposed the Family Assistance Plan, a program that for the first time would have extended cash income maintenance payments to working poor families with children. In April 1970, a bill incorporating the major features of the Family Assistance Plan passed the House of Representatives by a vote of 243 to 155. It never passed the Senate, where it was crushed in the Finance Committee by an alliance of the most conservative and most liberal members against the middle-of-the-roaders. The fascinating political story of this proposed legislation is ably told in Moynihan's recent book, *The Politics of a Guaranteed Income* (1973).

Long before income maintenance for the working poor was a bill or a presidential program, it was an idea advanced by prominent economists. Milton Friedman first proposed the negative income tax; James Tobin, Joseph Pechman, and Robert Lampman were among those who advocated it and helped to explore its mechanics and its impact.

In June 1967, the Office of Economic Opportunity funded an experiment designed to test the effects of negative income tax payments on the labor supply of low-wage workers in metropolitan areas in New Jersey and Pennsylvania. The experiment was conducted jointly by the Institute for Research on Poverty of the University of Wisconsin and by Mathematica, a research firm with headquarters in Princeton, New Jersey. The test lasted three years and involved 1,357 low-income families in Trenton, Paterson, Passaic, Jersey City, and Scranton. Of these families, 725 were eligible to receive negative income tax payments by check every two weeks, and 632 were untreated controls. Both experimental and control families were interviewed at length every three months. The sample included roughly equal numbers of black, white, and Spanish-speaking families, in proportions that varied across the sites. Almost all were husband-wife families, with an average of about six members. The average payment to a husband-wife family was about $24 per week, though some families received much more.

The labor supply results of the New Jersey–Pennsylvania experiment have now become available. They show quite small reductions in labor supply for the experimental in comparison to the control families — an overall reduction of not more than 10 percent, and probably much closer to 5 percent. This reduction came about largely because some experimental husbands shortened their hours of work, because some wives left paid employment to devote more time to work in their homes, and because some husbands looked for work longer when they became unemployed. None of the reduction in labor supply occurred in black families — for these families the payments had no measurable effect in reducing labor market work.

It is also of interest that the experimental treatment did not appear to have many measurable impacts on the life-style or the attitudes of the experimental families. More of them became homeowners or moved into more expensive rented dwelling units, and they bought more major appliances than the control group; but in most other respects, there were no discernible differences.

The New Jersey–Pennsylvania experiment cannot, of course, be regarded as conclusive. Fortunately, even larger income maintenance experiments are now under way in three other metropolitan areas: Denver, Seattle, and Gary (Indiana). However, the New Jersey–Pennsylvania results strongly suggest that a negative income tax would not have the large effects on labor supply predicted by some nonexperimental statistical studies, or alleged by the political foes of the Family Assistance Plan. In view of these promising results, one might hope that new legislative proposals for income maintenance will soon be forthcoming — and will fare better than the Family Assistance Plan did. Moreover, the New Jersey–Pennsylvania experiment shows that deliberate experimentation, with random assignment of subjects to experimental and control groups, is a powerful method for evaluating the effects of social programs, including programs in the area of manpower and labor supply.

EVALUATING MANPOWER PROGRAMS

In the past decade, we have seen the initiation of a large number of manpower programs of different kinds, many of them designed to improve the skills of disadvantaged workers. Some have been judged failures and have disappeared. Most, however, are continuing or growing.

It is deplorable that after all this effort, we have so little hard evidence about how well these programs have succeeded. Which of them have helped low-wage workers become high-wage workers, and which have not? Which have led workers from intermittent to steady employment, or from menial to satisfying work? Which kinds of workers have been helped most, and why? Which programs should be expanded, and which curtailed? Such questions remain largely matters of opinion and controversy.

The problem is not the lack of evaluative studies by qualified social scientists. There have been many such studies, competently done. On the whole, the researchers have used sophisticated statistical methods far more powerful than the simple descriptive statistics that were used by most labor economists of my generation. But they all suffer from one basic defect: They are retrospective — done after the fact. After a program is completed, the analyst conducting a cost-benefit study somehow locates a control group that did not go through the program and compares it with the graduates or program completers.

The use of control groups selected in this way must always be subject to suspicion. Those eligible for a program who do not enter it will inevitably differ from those who do. Those who drop out will differ from those who finish. These differences cannot be fully captured by standardization or matching on such measurable characteristics as age, race, or years of school completed. In consequence, if such a post hoc study shows benefits from the program, one will inevitably remain in doubt whether the measured benefits are real or statistical artifacts.

The cure for these doubts is of course the true experiment. The best way to get a convincing and unbiased test of a manpower program is to make a random assignment of applicants or eligibles to treated and control groups and to do a longitudinal study of both groups that begins before the program begins and continues after it ends.

Such true experiments are expensive when compared to nonexperimental studies that use such data bases as Social Security records. For this reason, studies based on existing data bases should be continued and strengthened, since they can provide data on much larger numbers of trainees and nontrainees than the more powerful, but more limited experiments. Nevertheless, true experiments are cheap, compared to the total expenditure on manpower programs. If they help us decide how and where manpower funds can be spent most effectively in the future, they would be well worth their cost.

The more serious problem of a true experiment is that the need for random assignment deprives the program administrator of the right to make a judgmental selection of trainees. He or she may want to select the most trainable, so that the program will succeed; or the administrator may want to select the most deserving or the neediest so that the program will do the most good. In either case, he or she seriously biases any program evaluation that compares trainees with nontrainees. Random assignment may seem to the program administrator to be unethical in denying treatment to those most in need, or unprofessional in denying him or her the right to exercise judgment in selecting trainees.

Given these attitudes on the part of vocational educators and training directors, it will seldom be possible first to fund a training or counseling program and then to insist on experimental evaluation of it. Rather the experimental evaluation must be made a precondition of program funding. Where it is necessary or desirable to include all of the neediest or most trainable workers in a program in order to achieve program objectives, it is still possible to do a limited true experiment by randomly assigning workers to treatment and control groups in a range of incomes or test scores near the margin of eligibility for entry into the program, while including all those well below the margin. Such scientific evaluation of manpower programs could be of great benefit in helping us decide how best to assist the low-wage worker in the years ahead.

THE JOURNEY TO WORK

As the size of major metropolitan areas grows, more and more time is spent by workers commuting to and from their jobs. Old public transportation systems become increasingly unsuited to the changing locations of work, lose patronage, and must raise fares. Often they have become much less pleasant and less safe than they once were. The chief sufferers from the decline of the public transportation system are low-wage workers, who are most dependent on it to get to their jobs.

Most studies of commuting problems have been done by transportation economists and urban planners. Labor economists as such have been relatively uninvolved. Yet there are many important relationships among the journey to work, the behavior of the work force, and the conditions of the workplace.

Workers must somehow be compensated for the cost of commuting in time, fare, and inconvenience. One form of compensation is the lower cost of high-quality housing as one moves away from the central business district to areas where land rents are lower. In the days when almost all white-collar work was in the central business district, most of the costs of commuting by white-collar workers could have been compensated through lower housing costs. Now, however, white-collar employment opportunities are increasing in the suburbs. Moreover, suburban land values may be rising relative to values in central cities. One therefore would expect that central business district employers will need to pay a wage premium to attract suburban workers in some white-collar occupations. In other words, some of the incidence of commuting costs will be shifted to central business district employers. Conversely public subsidies of mass transit systems would tend to limit the rise of wages in central cities.

For blue-collar workers, employment has never been concentrated in central business districts. It has been widely dispersed in most metropolitan areas. Thus much of the incidence of commuting to the less accessible portions of metropolitan areas should long ago have been reflected in wages. This may be one of the major reasons for pay differentials by establishment size, since the larger an establishment, the less adequate will be the labor supply in its immediate neighborhood and the greater its need to employ workers who must commute long distances.

Relatively little research has been done relating labor market variables, such as occupation and wage level, to the journey to work in terms of distance traveled and mode of transportation used. More work along these lines could have important implications both for labor market and for transportation policies. Offner (1972) has shown that in New York City, even relatively small differences in distances to job concentrations have significant effects on the labor force participation rates of ghetto residents. This research was based on census data. One can imagine similar studies that would use richer bodies of data which come from surveys of employees and personnel records of employers. Such studies could be helpful in evaluating proposals to subsidize mass transit systems.

The desirability of reducing commuting time also lies behind the recent movements toward changing the length and timing of the workweek. The four-day workweek is still in its infancy, and little information is available on how well it works. Studies of the firms that use it would be most welcome. However, the increasing number of paid holidays means many four-day workweeks, even for workers who ordinarily work five days a week.

The decreasing number of workdays per year in turn exacerbates the problems of public transit systems, which must maintain services on weekends and holidays for a smaller number of riders. The fewer the days with full loads, the higher the fares must be. Perhaps the proper solution is to have more holidays that are not the same for everyone — the worker's own birthday or his wife's (her husband's) instead of Abraham Lincoln's or Martin Luther King's. Such staggered holidays reduce congestion without underusing the available transit resources. Creative thinking is needed about this range of problems — to call it research may be dignifying it unduly.

COMPENSATING WAGE DIFFERENTIALS

Few propositions in economics have a longer history than the proposition that unpleasant jobs should command a wage premium, for it was set forth clearly by Adam Smith (1937, p. 100) in 1776:

> The wages of labour vary with the ease or hardship, the cleanliness or dirtyness, the honourableness or dishonourableness

of the employment. . . . The trade of a butcher is a brutal and odious business; but it is in most places more profitable than the greater part of common trades. The most detestable of all employments, that of public executioner, is, in proportion to work done, better paid than any common trade whatever.

Yet in recent years, many unpleasant jobs in metropolitan labor markets have *not* been well rewarded. Dishwashers, garbage collectors, and others in similarly disagreeable jobs have been among the lowest paid. Is Adam Smith's principle wrong? Not necessarily. However, it has been counterbalanced in modern America by two forces that did not exist in eighteenth century Britain: demand deficiency unemployment and racial discrimination in employment. If people have been unemployed for a long time, they will accept low wages for disagreeable work rather than have no work at all. If blacks, Puerto Ricans, and chicanos are kept out of agreeable jobs by discrimination, there will be an excess supply of labor to disagreeable jobs that will keep their wages low.

For a variety of reasons, I think that this state of affairs may be changing. An obvious reason is the successful unionization of workers in some disagreeable jobs. In New York City, the garbage collector makes 90 percent of the pay of a police officer or a firefighter. Moreover, he has a splendid new title to match his pay — he is a uniformed sanitation man. Even in cities with weaker municipal unions — there are surely few with stronger — other forces may be contributing to this outcome. A reduction in the migration flow from rural to metropolitan areas is an inevitable consequence of the relative decline in rural population. This must mean a smaller supply of labor willing to accept the least agreeable urban jobs at low wages. To the extent that legislation promoting equal employment opportunities for minorities succeeds in achieving its objectives, some low-wage workers from minority groups will have better opportunities open to them. This, too, will reduce the supply of labor to disagreeable jobs.

If we look back over the entire period since 1900, it is clear that pay differentials between skilled and unskilled work have decreased substantially. As the flow of unskilled immigrants from Europe, the rural South, and Puerto Rico has diminished, the wages for disagreeable, unskilled work have risen relative to the wages of craftsmen and white-collar workers. It is not impossible that in another generation, unskilled workers in disagreeable jobs will typically get higher pay than some skilled workers in "agreeable" jobs. We are no longer in a position where the demand for educated workers is growing faster than the supply. The least skilled hospital workers in New York City have recently received a wage increase of 6 percent. Only a few academic employees will gain that much at the present time, not because there are any restrictions against it, but because their employers can't afford it and have no trouble in filling vacancies.

I suggest as part of our research agenda that we need more up-to-date studies of the movement of skills differentials and better studies than have yet been done of other kinds of wage differentials and the forces that produce them. To support such research, we need much more systematic collection of occupational wage rates. At present, our system of wage data relies heavily on average hourly earnings by industry, and occupational wage rates are collected only for a small segment of the entire employed work force.

The low-wage worker has long been a serious social problem, and still is. However, I am unpersuaded that a depressed secondary labor market is an inevitable feature of American capitalism. A free enterprise economy with full employment and without discrimination in employment could perhaps wipe out much of the present low-wage, dead-end job syndrome. It may be prudent to find out more about the trends now in progress and to reinforce them with effective, yet moderate, reforms before we advocate radical change.

REFERENCES

Moynihan, Daniel P. *The Politics of a Guaranteed Income: The Nixon Administration and the Family Assistance Plan.* New York: Random House. 1973.

Offner, Paul. "Labor Force Participation in the Ghetto." *Journal of Human Resources* (1972).

Piore, Michael Joseph. "Notes for a Theory of Labor Market Stratification." Working paper no. 95. Cambridge, Massachusetts: M.I.T., Department of Economics. October 1972.

Smith, Adam. *The Wealth of Nations.* Book I, chapter X. New York: Modern Library. 1937.

Welch, Finis. "Minimum Wage Legislation in the United States." Washington, D.C.: U.S. Department of Labor, Office of Policy, Evaluation and Research. July 1973. Unpublished paper.

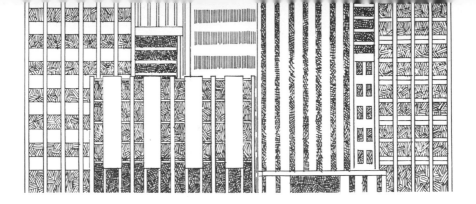

8
Directions for a Research Strategy

ELI GINZBERG*

There are underlying assumptions about the metropolis, some of which dominate both the public's and the specialists' views of what is wrong with our large cities from the vantage point of providing employment and income opportunities for their populations. Among these are:

(1) There is insufficiency of jobs for all who are able and willing to work.

(2) A large number of jobs pay so poorly that they do not enable the incumbents to support their families on their earnings.

(3) Many families live under dysfunctional conditions which diminish their lives and prevent the development of their children's potential.

(4) Serious inequities exist among different groups which tend to persist, despite our society's commitment to equality and opportunity.

(5) There is growing unease that those trapped in the city's slums will not be able to extricate themselves, even with the passage of time.

These gloomy assumptions can lead to urban passivity and inaction and thereby they lead to a self-fulfilling prophecy. No city assuredly can

* A. Barton Hepburn professor of economics, Graduate School of Business, and director, Conservation of Human Resources, Columbia University.

look to time alone to cure its ills. It must organize to make better decisions today so that a better future can emerge. Admittedly, cities are part of an open economy and society and as such are exposed to many forces over which they have little or no direct control, forces emanating from their state capitals, from the District of Columbia, from a myriad of corporate decisions, even from the actions of King Faisal and the Shah of Iran.

However, even if cities are unable to set their own course and pursue it without reference to these powerful forces, they constantly have opportunities to respond to what is happening on both the inside and the outside — and how they respond is not preordained. The more the leadership of a city is able to articulate its plans for the future, the more it can secure a broad consensus that supports these goals, the more effective its decision-making apparatus, the greater influence it will be able to exert over its own destiny. The beginning, if not the end of a research strategy for the metropolis must focus on these basics. An urban leadership must instill in the public the conviction that it can affect its own future through cooperative action, the leadership must gain agreement as to the principal goals the city should seek to achieve, and the decision-making machinery must be such that these goals can be realized. These three preconditions are essential to the vitalizing of urban decision making. Unless they exist, there is little prospect that a research strategy will have much success. But to the extent that they are in place, progress along the axes discussed below can prove supportive.

FRAMEWORK FOR A STRATEGY

The framework which follows has been developed to facilitate the ordering of the diverse suggestions advanced about how the crucial questions concerning manpower and the metropolis can best be investigated. The classificatory schema contains a number of categories (in order) to facilitate review and assessment. Briefly, these classifications are:

(1) *Methodological considerations:* Explores the extent to which all studies of the metropolis are constrained by the existing data base and determines the potential for strengthening it

(2) *Historical and comparative analyses:* Calls attention to the new and deeper insights which can be gained by looking at cities from these perspectives

(3) *Employer behavior:* Underscores the fact that decisions made by the private sector can influence, for good or bad, the future of the metropolitan area

(4) *Public policy and programming:* Emphasizes that we live in a pluralistic economy and society and that the shape of every city's future will be materially affected by the quality of the decisions made in the public arena at every level of government

(5) *Research in relation to policy:* Raises a set of considerations about the current and potential impact of new knowledge in improving decision making over the entire range of policy arenas — private, nonprofit, or governmental

(6) *Potentialities and limitations of planning:* Involves an effort to sort out the decisions which can best be left to the individual or to the nuclear family and the arenas where communal and government planning is essential if the city is to progress

Practical Application of the Strategy

To recapitulate — three of the categories are rooted in the research arena dealing respectively with methodological considerations (1), historical and comparative analyses (2), and research in relation to policy (5); while the other three — employer behavior (3), public policy and programming (4), and potentialities and limitations of planning (6) — fall primarily into the policy realm. But once these distinctions are made, the reader must remember that the classification schema is primarily one of convenience and that the conceptual and analytical ties between the two major subdivisions (research and policy) and among the six categories remain to be clarified.

Methodological Considerations

The way in which the Census Bureau collects and publishes data concerning central cities and their suburban rings, places of residence and employment, and the distance of the journey to work was found to overdetermine the manner in which students are able to analyze the interactions between manpower resources and metropolitan economies. The present flow of materials must be broadened and deepened and above all refined if analysts are to be able to explore the complex changes occurring with respect to where people live and work and how they commute to work. Among the most serious shortcomings of the present data are the geographic criteria used to distinguish the central city from neighboring counties. These criteria do not permit one to distinguish sharply the intensity of economic activity in each area and the flows of people, jobs, and income among these areas.

Difficulties also exist when it comes to probing the residential, employment, and income characteristics of the inner city, especially in the case of our largest metropolitan centers which do not represent a single labor market but rather a number of loosely interdependent labor markets, depending on patterns of industrial concentration, housing, and the availability of transportation.

Considering the predominant role that the metropolitan economy has come to play, there is a twofold requirement: The Census Bureau should explore how it can reform its data collection so that the information it collects can better illuminate changes in the dynamics of metropolitan economies. At the same time the research community must address itself to studying several labor markets within the central city and the suburban rings and the interactions among them. With a few notable exceptions, this arena of research remains *terra incognita*.

Both private and public decision makers have need for better guidance concerning the future directions of the demand and supply for manpower within the metropolitan area. Admittedly there are inherent difficulties in the use of any type of forecasting model, if only because of the openness of the city in terms of the people who are free to move in or move out. Still, such movements, especially in the near and intermediate term (five to seven years), are not likely to be of an order of magnitude to vitiate projections which restrict themselves to directions and first-order magnitudes.

Among the approaches that warrant exploration are efforts focused on disaggregating a macro model and, in the process, taking account of the most probable deviations of the metropolitan region. So long as the objectives of this disaggregation approach are geared to delineating broad directions and first-order magnitudes, the explorations may well be justified.

A related effort would be to construct a matrix of the most important metropolitan industry and occupational patterns on the assumption that these are likely to show considerable stability in the short and intermediate periods. Hence if one could estimate the fast and slower growing (and declining) sectors of the metropolitan economy, it would be possible to get a first fix on the types of manpower which might be in relatively short supply and on where potential surpluses are likely to occur. Again, it should be emphasized that such an approach, even if successful, could do little more than provide some general directions to policy makers in the private and public sectors. However, such general directions geared to near-term developments might prove quite useful.

In the face of the present paucity of metropolitan manpower data, it might be well for governmental and nongovernmental specialists to take another look at the area-skill surveys to determine whether these might not be improved to a point where they could help fill part of the void. Admittedly, the conventional approach of asking employers about their hiring intentions some months hence would have to be refined before the results could be useful. But in the absence of clear-cut alternatives to assessing metropolitan manpower developments, it is questionable whether even this admittedly imperfect approach should be discarded before one more effort is made to shore it up.

Still another recommendation points to designing a sample of key employers of varying sizes and occupational mixes and monitoring their employment changes with an aim of extrapolating from their experience to the larger community. Once again, it must be recognized that decision makers have need for broad as well as specific data and that such a structured sample study might provide them with information as to the broad directions of metropolitan manpower developments.

There is no basis for optimism that any of these approaches will yield significant new understanding of major metropolitan manpower developments. But unless a serious research effort is made to explore how the existing lacunae about basic manpower facts and trends can be reduced, there is little prospect that our large cities will be able to improve the quality of their decision-making processes.

Major demographic changes are under way which carry with them important implications for the future of our large cities. More attention should be focused on such a question as: To what extent can the nation's large cities look forward to a substantial reduction, even a potential drying up, of the streams of poor whites and poor blacks undertaking to migrate from farm areas? The surplus population left on the farms has greatly diminished. At the same time, consideration must be paid to the millions of underemployed and low-income earners now living in rural nonfarm places and to the likelihood of their becoming the principal source of future migrants to the city.

There is considerable evidence of a new pattern of internal migration consisting of people moving from one city to another. What are the magnitudes of these city-to-city movements? More particularly, what are the conditions which accelerate or retard such movements? And finally, what subgroups in the population are most likely to be found among these migrants?

Conventional wisdom holds that once their children are grown, many suburbanites move back into the central city. Is this a fact? And are the numbers involved of sufficient magnitude to be an important factor in the future well-being of the central city?

What are the intermediate and long-term implications of a continuing and rapid decline in national and urban fertility? Is there a real threat in these population trends that many large cities will be unable to maintain their existing population base? What does a more slowly growing urban population imply for reducing some of the disabilities associated with urban density? More particularly, is there any likelihood that the combined declines of in-migration and lowered fertility will result in a constriction of certain metropolitan labor markets so that it will be difficult for the central city inhabitants to maintain their existing level of economic activity?

To what extent will certain cities which serve as ports of entry — such as New York, Miami, San Antonio, New Orleans, Los Angeles, San Francisco — continue to attract large numbers of illegal immigrants who will find a place in the interstices of these labor markets?

The "urban problem" of the last two decades has been explained largely in terms of racial and ethnic difficulties growing out of the exchange of populations, with middle-class whites moving to the suburbs and poorly educated and low-skill minorities moving into the inner city. In light of the fact that half of all blacks now reside outside the South and that they, the same as whites, are experiencing rapidly falling birthrates, are the exacerbated racial conflicts of the past two decades in northern and western cities likely to moderate on the ground of demography alone?

Another line of inquiry that invites research effort concerns the extent to which economic events on the national and international scene will determine our large cities' future levels of employment, income, and well-being. Greater analytic efforts are required to delineate the areas within which different types of cities are able to influence the multitude of economic forces playing upon them both from within and from without. With the economy of New York City tied (if only to a minor degree) to economic developments in Tokyo, Rio de Janeiro, and Johannesburg, those in decision-making positions must be aware of and responsive to such far-flung linkages.

The energy crisis has pointed up the necessity for a better understanding among the ways in which jobs, transportation, and the labor force are interrelated. If schools are unable to operate five days a week because of a shortage of fuel, many mothers currently in the labor force may be forced to stay at home to look after their children.

Another methodological weakness which limits understanding, planning, and decision making in large cities grows out of the sparsity of longitudinal data. There is a widespread belief that cities are major transformers of manpower, taking in poorly educated and trained people whose offspring, after one or two generations of improved schooling and employment, are enabled to move up the ladder. Most of the information available about the poor and near-poor, in-migrants, and minority group members is cross-sectional. We know a good deal about social pathology and human deprivation as of one point in time. But we need to know much more about what happens to families on an intergenerational basis. Such knowledge is not easy to garner, but it is not beyond the reach of modern research capabilities. It is also crucial if the vast expenditures on health, education, welfare, and other social services are to be more effectively directed to the groups most in need of special assistance.

Another data problem that emerges is the need for students of urban affairs to recognize the limitations of the economist's approach when he is assessing the well-being of a metropolitan community. The economist looks at wages almost solely through the mechanism of the price system where they serve as an allocative device. However, in the context of urban development and well-being, wages must also be related to family structure and need. A job at the minimum wage may be a satisfactory opening position for a seventeen-year-old high school dropout living at home; it is unsatisfactory for a head of household with three dependents. In short, social scientists must learn to regroup the data about the city and its people in many different ways in order to assess their many meanings.

Let us return to the example of wages. Wages provide a key measure of labor costs. But they also must be assessed from the vantage of the local cost of living; the manner in which they attract or discourage various groups of potential workers, i.e., youth and married women; the role they play in race relations; and the way in which they are interrelated with welfare standards and still other aspects of the city's life and well-being.

One more methodological issue: The cities have been and will certainly continue to be major arenas of social experimentation involving efforts to improve education, health, welfare, social security, race relations, and other crucial aspects of contemporary life. There is a vast need for researchers to become engaged in a much greater degree than heretofore in the design and evaluation of such experiments, for unless they do, taxpayers will remain in the dark about the outcomes. One can additionally say that the research community faces an even broader challenge of exploring how it might help design outcome measures so that the routine expenditures of local governments can be more effectively assessed. With local governments responsible for the expenditure of ever larger sums — in New York City local government accounts for about a quarter of the income of the population — the establishment and use of outcome measures for public services are urgently needed if the elected and appointed officials are not to continue to make decisions solely on the basis of sheer political pressure exerted upon them.

These are some of the more important areas in which new and improved data and studies are required if the quality of metropolitan decision making is to be enhanced. The remedies will not come easily or cheaply, since our strongest data base is national rather than metropolitan and since our social scientists are conditioned to studying macro issues and are relatively unsophisticated in approaching problems on a metropolitan level. Yet a major shift is urgently required, for to a large extent the future well-being of our cities depends upon a strengthening of their informational and decision-making mechanisms.

Historical and Comparative Studies

A second important avenue for progress in metropolitan studies is through historical and comparative analyses. There is no single prototype of a large city. The largest urban agglomerations are characterized by a high degree of diversity, reinforced by the size and diversity of the country of which they are a part. With the single exception of the U.S.S.R., the United States is the only industrialized nation in the world of continental scale. This suggests the need for caution in drawing comparisons between American cities and the principal European cities — i.e., London, Paris, Rome, Amsterdam, Brussels, Stockholm, each of which is a national capital of a relatively small country with a much more homogeneous population. One need only name some of our largest cities — New York, Chicago, Los Angeles, Houston, Detroit — to appreciate the need to study them in sufficient depth to capture their uniqueness which, at a minimum, encompasses marked differences in ethnic and racial distributions, industrial structure, political leadership, and cultural ambience.

Much the same point about diversity and uniqueness can be made about our suburban areas; i.e., the perimeters of our large metropolitan centers. Here, too, there is need for developing a typology which would group these areas according to whether they are growing or have leveled off; whether they are centers of manufacturing or primarily bedroom communities; whether they have reached a size where they are well on the way to becoming satellite cities; or whether they are, at the opposite extreme, highly restricted residential areas for the upper middle class and the wealthy. The contention here advanced does not speak against aggregative analysis, but it does point up the need for disaggregation as a first step. Unless researchers proceed in this fashion, they run the risk of dealing with such heterogeneous aggregations that they will unwittingly wash out most of the details that contain within themselves the explanatory power to account for metropolitan changes.

In addition to putative gains from well-structured comparative analyses, there is need for more historical studies. Despite the contemporary bias in favor of econometric analyses, historical investigations can make a useful contribution to the understanding of urban dynamics by highlighting some of the mechanisms that had earlier helped transform the urban economy and population. It is still moot whether the urban poor today face comparable or different conditions from the urban poor of the middle and late nineteenth century. Clearly the labor markets have changed, but so has access to the preparatory institutions. Earlier, the poor were immigrants from western, central, or southern Europe; now they are likely to be black. But how much importance should be ascribed to this difference? And what about the increased opportunities for today's women to work out of the home? Does this imply an earlier escape of families from poverty?

While one should not look to history to answer the more complex issues of contemporary metropolitan life, it is hard to see how a deeper understanding of the evolution of our older cities can fail to illuminate their present condition and to offer some clues as to the directions in which they are headed.

Employer Behavior

The next rubric under which research suggestions can be formulated relates to the behavior of employers. Two points should be noted: Academicians have been slow to explore and exploit this arena for research purposes, in part because of a generic distrust of what goes on in the profit-seeking sector, but equally important, because those who have sought to use corporate data have encountered serious and often impassable obstacles in gaining access to the records or in gaining permission to publish their findings.

However, past difficulties do not justify future neglect. Corporate behavior provides a major clue to the understanding of urban dynamics. One specific advantage of looking at the forces that impinge on the employer and at how he deals with them is a sharpened focus on the decision-making process, albeit at a micro level. But many micros may provide a first clue to the macro scene. We know that more and more central city employers — particularly banks, department stores, utilities, hotels and restaurants, hospitals, and many others — have been forced to adapt their manpower and personnel policies and practices to the new urban labor force. Hence a study of their adaptations would provide a needed interfacing of manpower and the metropolis. The research challenge is twofold: first, to develop some case studies in depth concerning those adaptations whereby employers have sought to deal more effectively with their new labor sources, and second, to look for significant generalizations underlying this variegated experience.

A second aspect of employer behavior that invites study relates to the matrix of forces that plays upon their decision to remain in the city or to move out, and more particularly, the extent to which the question of manpower resources influences the outcome. Many stories make the rounds that various firms which have moved from a central business district over the last few years have done so because they were unable to meet their manpower requirements. They simply could not get the trained personnel they needed. Or a variant thereof stresses the difficulties firms faced from their own staffs because of their urban location. Occasionally the stories also refer to adverse labor costs in the form of high wage structures; more generally the emphasis is on low productivity and trade union constraints. But for the most part complaints center on the difficulties of attracting and retaining an adequate supply of competent people.

It may well be that difficulties anchored in the manpower arena explain the flight of many large and small entrepreneurs from the city center; however, in the absence of carefully executed investigations, to accept this conclusion is an act of faith.

The fact that there is more to the story is reinforced by two newspaper accounts on the same day, in late 1973 : Cities Service was leaving New York City to consolidate its headquarters in Tulsa, while Delta Airlines was relocating a large number of its executives in New York City so that it could be closer to where the action was. Economists have no difficulty in recognizing that two large companies — one an integrated oil firm, the other a large airline — may reach diametrically opposite conclusions about the advantages of a particular metropolitan location. But if our understanding of urban dynamics is to be deepened, what we need are not generalized models but studies in depth, so that the role of the interacting variables can be correctly assessed.

Since some large companies unquestionably will continue to leave the central business district to relocate in the suburban ring or in smaller cities, the principles that guide their relocation should be a matter of both academic and public concern. If a large national corporation accepts without protest the practices prevailing in a community where it may consider relocating, it may reinforce discriminatory patterns in employment and housing. On the other hand, if it is determined to use its bargaining strength to the full, it can lean against such discriminatory patterns by making their abolition a precondition for its relocation. The fact that minority groups have taken several large corporations to court to stop their flight from the racially mixed central city to outlying white enclaves adds relevance to these considerations. If the courts should decide that such relocation jeopardizes the constitutional rights of those presently on the payroll, the tradeoffs between staying and leaving the city may change radically. In any case, here is yet another unexplored aspect of the interfacing of manpower and the metropolis.

There are two further facets of employer behavior which warrant attention. For the last decade the federal government has been expanding its funding for manpower training and related services in order to assist the hard-to-employ more effectively in linking them to the labor market. In the last few years the Labor Department has been moving in the direction of decentralizing responsibility for planning and implementation to the states and localities, a move which will accelerate now that Congress has passed the 1973 Comprehensive Employment and

Training Act. There is a great deal that employers may be able to do cooperatively via consortia and other devices to put these training monies to more effective use in helping the poorly educated inner city labor force prepare for current job openings. A careful search will reveal several such cooperative experiments. These should be assessed and the lessons extracted so that future plans can be strengthened. In our largest metropolitan communities more attention should be focused on the potential of employers — including those in the not-for-profit sector — in the same or adjacent neighborhoods for entering cooperative training, placement, and upgrading efforts, as for instance, becoming constituents of an educational park or a medical center.

The multiple interdependencies that underlie the large city point to yet another arena where employer behavior may offer constructive opportunities for action and study. To illustrate: The ability of employers to attract workers, particularly in off hours, may depend on heightened security, improved transportation, and the availability of local services; e.g., eating places. It may not be feasible for any one employer, even a large one, to create the conditions which would assure him of the workers he needs; yet cooperative action among a group of employers in the same area may prove successful. Cooperative efforts of this nature should be reviewed and assessed. Moreover, analysis should be directed to the possible impact of a radical change in conventional working practices, such as a reduction to the four-day workweek. Clearly there are a great many different fronts on which urban employers interact with the metropolitan labor force, and there is a great deal we still need to learn about these relationships.

Public Policy and Programming

The next grouping relates to the arena of public policy and planning, critical factors in shaping the future of our major metropolitan communities. To begin with, one must note that municipal governments are spending large sums on human betterment and that in a political democracy such spending inevitably reflects the distribution of political power. Yet the researcher has a contribution to make by helping to sharpen the goals of such interaction, delineate the preferred methods of pursuing them, and engage in the critical assessment of results.

Major efforts have been under way to assess the impact of income supplementation on incentives to work. The fact that the Office of Economic Opportunity demonstrations were carefully planned and that care was taken in selecting participants and controls suggests that the findings, when they become available, may provide the American people with the type of guidance they so badly need when it comes to assessing the costs and benefits of social intervention.

The size of the country and the diversity of its people and problems speak to the desirability, and in fact necessity, of our experimenting carefully before entering upon large new programs of social intervention. The only possible way for legislators and the public to secure the necessary guidance and feedback is for trial efforts to be made under a diversity of circumstances and for operating data systems to be put into place so that outcomes can be summarized and evaluated. The shortcomings of the Great Society programs were less in what they failed to accomplish and more in our failure to learn what worked, what didn't work, and why.

The problems of the city are compounded because of the high interdependencies that exist among such major subsystems as employment, housing, and transportation — to single out but three. While there may be good reasons why a government should hesitate to subsidize intra- or interurban transportation, no arguments from economics alone can settle the issue of subsidization *a priori* until one takes into account the implications for employment and income-earning opportunities that might be jeopardized if the transportation network of a large metropolitan area were permitted to fall apart. It requires both analysis and judgment to reach a balanced assessment of the short- and long-term consequences of such subsidization.

A related area concerns the policy to be pursued with respect to abandoned or about-to-be abandoned land. Since land is the basic limiting resource of all cities, how it is handled will have a major impact on the metropolis's future. Here, too, there are likely to be difficult trade-offs between social benefits and social costs. Admittedly, real estate interests keep looking to government for actions that will facilitate their making windfall profits. But if the city neglects to put together parcels of the abandoned land and if it fails to offer various inducements to bring such land back into productive use, it may erode its economic and employment base. It does not follow that help to real estate promoters is necessarily faulty public policy.

Large cities are not only large employers, accounting for about 15 percent of all urban jobs, they are also the dispensers of transfer payments which provide essential income to large numbers of people who are not working but who might, under supportive arrangements, be able to work. One of the challenges large cities should meet is to explore how some of the transfer income under their control might be used to encourage potential employables to get off welfare and into productive work, even if the municipal authorities must initially establish both the job opportunities and the ancillary support these disadvantaged groups require. There is nothing easy about going down this road, but there is also nothing easy about the city's continuing to support large numbers of potentially employable adults in idleness. Since most municipalities have a great amount of public work that needs doing, the conversion of persons on welfare into productive workers commends itself, surely on an experimental basis.

There is a widespread belief that the large city is an inhospitable environment for manufacturing, especially in an era of heightened concern about pollution and other environmental dangers. But those directly concerned with the economic welfare of the city worry every time a manufacturing unit closes down its operations and relocates. The right kinds of manufacturing can provide good jobs and clean jobs which can be absorbed safely within the city's borders. We simply have not studied adequately the types of manufacturing employment that have moved from our large metropolitan centers together with the considerable flow of new, if different, manufacturing jobs that have moved in. Once again, gross categories hide more than they reveal.

Since so many of our large cities' problems are directly or indirectly related to racial and ethnic discrimination, more attention should be directed to identifying the high costs in terms of losses of efficiency and equity that derive from the persistence of discrimination and how accelerated programs can be made to lower these barriers which hobble the progress of both individuals and the community.

The city's future also will be affected by developments from the outside. The future of the suburbs is one such important determinant. Students need to learn more about the protection of the suburban turf. If the suburbs continue to be controlled by the affluent who place a high price on an environment in which to live, they will slow use of land for industrial and commercial purposes and will seek to prevent housing being erected for low-income groups. To the extent that the affluent succeed, the expansion of the suburbs will be seriously constrained, thereby contributing indirectly to the future vitality of the city. We need to know much more about the relative strength of various interest groups that will in the long run influence so greatly the economic future of our cities by determining what happens to our suburbs.

Another external parameter is the strength and direction of national economic policy. No city can solve its manpower and economic problems and assure its future unless the federal government succeeds in pursuing policies that are simultaneously supportive of national economic growth and nondiscriminatory against the nation's largest cities. More analysis is required of the interplay between federal policies and metropolitan well-being. There is a conviction, surely among the mayors of our largest cities, that the federal government has not dealt fairly with them. The argument has less to do with abstract justice and more with delineating the principal problems our large cities face that cannot be solved except with substantial federal assistance. Clearly, if our national unemployment rate goes to 6 percent and more, there is little any large city can do to assure employment opportunities for all of its members. Here the city clearly depends upon the federal government. But what is less clear is how the malfunctioning of many ghetto schools is to be overcome by federal action. More funds would help, but only the optimist believes that more money is the key.

The probable emergence of a much improved state fiscal position resulting from revenue sharing and declining rates of population growth calls attention to a third external parameter which will affect the future of our large cities. The challenge that our largest cities face is to develop alliances with other urban communities in their state and with their neighboring suburbs, many of which are searching for an increased share of state aid. While such coalition building is primarily the task of the politician, here, too, the analyst can be of help by exploring the extent to which the difficult problems first encountered by the large city are emerging increasingly in smaller cities and many larger suburbs. It is probably not true that the problems of the large city are unique. They only appear to be for reasons of scale.

The thrust of these considerations has been to highlight the many dimensions of public policy and programming and to point out how a stronger data base, better analyses, and carefully controlled experiments can contribute to better decision making. Admittedly, decisions are currently being made and must continue to be made in the absence of adequate information and knowledge; but that should only encourage the researcher to increase his contribution.

Research in Relation to Policy

Our focus now shifts to an overt consideration of the relationship between research and policy which has run through all of the preceding sections and which was close to the surface in the discussions of public policy and programming just completed.

The first point that warrants attention is the need in all metropolitan studies to make room for the individual, as a source of information and as the recipient of feedback from completed studies. The simple fact is that no study can have a positive effect on outcomes unless the findings are understood and accepted by those who must eventually act on them. To clarify this point: If the majority of the people living in a neighborhood are determined not to move and are organized to back up their determination, there is little purpose in city officials' proceeding very far with a planning study about alternative land use which hinges on the inhabitants' relocation.

A closely related reason the individual must be a principal center of any research effort flows from the fact that our large metropolitan centers contain large numbers who do not necessarily share the dominant value system. Accordingly, studies predicated on rationalistic economic theorizing are likely to lead to erroneous results if they fail to allow for the specific cultural values determining the behavior of a particular group. It is no use to point out to young black girls that they can earn a good wage as a domestic. They will not accept employment as a maid no matter what the wage analysis shows. They have not waited 350 years for their long-delayed revolution only to accept what in their eyes is degrading work.

Another shortcoming of much policy research grows out of the fact that the investigator does not ask himself ahead of time how the answers to the questions he raises will be used to affect policy. To make matters worse, many investigators fail to stop long enough to explore whether they have in fact defined an important problem. Clearly, if they slip at this initial point, there can be no recovery down the road: Good answers and good liaison with the policy maker will not suffice.

The politics of the metropolis is never static, and the recent reshuffling of population makes it more dynamic than ever. The new immigrants and their children are making strenuous efforts to organize themselves with an aim of exerting more leverage on their own lives and of expanding the opportunities available to them. They may not always succeed in advancing their own interests, but they are determined to keep trying; and no studies of the metropolitan environment should fail to take their strivings into account.

All urban research is seriously handicapped by the fact that social scientists have never developed sophisticated techniques for extracting information from people, and they are even more handicapped when it comes to extracting information from people who have a cautious if not hostile stance toward the larger society. We know from the 1970 census that we are unable to develop an accurate count of the population in large metropolitan centers, and that the undercount, especially among certain minority groups, has reached a distressingly high percentage. If we are unable to count the urban population, we are that much farther behind when it comes to understanding the values many live by, the ties that bind them to relatives and neighbors, and their plans and goals. Here is a major drawback to understanding the metropolis and shaping policies to improve its functioning. The inner lives of many of its inhabitants are shrouded from view; and in the place of knowledge, we operate with assumptions which are almost certain to be faulty, since they grow out of a different social experience.

If urban research is hobbled by these serious limitations stemming from cultural diversity and alienation, it suffers at the opposite extreme from a failure to have explored the many ramifications that flow from the fact that the urban environment is influenced not by local government alone but also by state and federal government and the fact that many of the difficulties the cities experience result from the nonarticulation among these three levels of government. To refer back to the weaknesses of many inner-city schools: The state is the responsible agency for assuring that all citizens have the opportunity to become educated. But it is the rare state that has acted in accordance with its constitutional authority to exert leverage on the larger cities that have failed to educate many pupils. The arena of intergovernmental relations and its import for improved urban decision making is a largely unexplored domain which warrants systematic analysis and evaluation.

Potentialities and Limitations of Planning

The final rubric relates to the role of planning in urban life. No city can survive, much less prosper, without planning. A great many decisions made today will have long-term consequences. The real challenge to urbanologists is to identify the range within which planning must take place and the locus of decision making. Over a wide area one must continue to rely on the individual and his family to make the crucial decisions relating to education, training, and employment. In the area of land use and transportation, clearly municipal government must be the final arbiter. And many decisions which transcend the individual's sphere and which need not necessarily be assumed by government fall within the domain of intermediary institutions, including employers, trade unions, educational and health agencies, and many others. Not only can research help to discriminate the roles of the different actors, it should also point up how improved articulation among them can make planning more effective.

Despite the large and, some might even say, horrendous problems our large cities face, it is important to recall that most people who live and work in the metropolitan area are able to take care of themselves, to plan their own lives, and to go about realizing their personal goals. Yet it is clear that if this sanguine assessment holds for the majority, there is a considerable minority that is not so situated, that lacks the capacity or the resources to plan for itself, and that requires help. One of the principal challenges that large cities face is to design programs of social intervention which are truly responsive to the needs of those who require help so that they can be assisted to become independent. The success of programs of social intervention should be measured by the numbers who are enabled to care for themselves and the speed with which they are enabled to do so.

To increase the ability of the urban population to cope with earning its livelihood, reliance can be placed on market mechanisms, so long as the leadership recognizes that the existing market structures are imperfect and that they fail, sometimes abysmally, to meet the minimum needs of some of the population. In short, while a city has every reason to rely on tested institutions, it must not ignore the challenge of building new institutions which will be more responsive to new or unmet needs and to improve the articulation among institutions, both old and new. Only thus can a city modernize its infrastructure and help assure that it is responsive to the challenges of today and the opportunities of tomorrow. Here, too, the student of urban affairs has a major task. He must help identify the institutions which need to be modified and the new ones which should be erected if the full potentialities of the city's human resources are to be developed and deployed.

The critical perception of the modern metropolis is the variability which characterizes its institutions and its inhabitants. At no point can one rely on gross diagnosis and traditional therapies. The repeated stress on research does not derive from an exaggerated respect for the potentialities of social science but rather from an appreciation of the shortcomings in the information base and analytic structures which handicap the search for solutions to urban problems. Clearly no one group can by itself find the answers, for the future of every large city depends on continuing accommodations among many different groups — accommodations that are rooted in political power, economic advantage, and cultural hegemony. But even in this complex environment, there is a place for the social investigator who can help narrow the differences among the contestants by substituting knowledge for opinion, reality for fantasy, the realizable for the ideal.

Index

165